Tammy Buchan

The
WORSHIP
MAZE
Finding a Style to Fit Your Church

PAUL BASDEN

InterVarsity Press
Downers Grove, Illinois

InterVarsity Press
P.O. Box 1400, Downers Grove, IL 60515
World Wide Web: www.ivpress.com
E-mail: mail@ivpress.com

InterVarsity Press® is the book-publishing division of InterVarsity Christian Fellowship/USA®, a student
movement active on campus at hundreds of universities, colleges and schools of nursing in the United States
of America, and a member movement of the International Fellowship of Evangelical Students. For
information about local and regional activities, write Public Relations Dept., InterVarsity Christian
Fellowship/USA, 6400 Schroeder Rd., P.O. Box 7895, Madison, WI 53707-7895.

All Scripture quotations, unless otherwise indicated, are taken from the Holy Bible, New International
Version®. NIV®. Copyright ©1973, 1978, 1984 by International Bible Society. Used by permission of
Zondervan Publishing House. All rights reserved.

The order of service on page 51 is taken from The Revised Common Lectionary, copyright 1992. Used with
the permission of Abingdon Press.

Cover photograph: Michael Goss

ISBN 0-8308-2204-6

Printed in the United States of America ∞

Library of Congress Cataloging-in-Publication Data
Basden, Paul, 1955-
    The worship maze: finding a style to fit your church/Paul
Basden.
      p.   cm.
    Includes bibliographical references.
    ISBN 0-8308-2204-6 (pbk.: alk. paper)
    1. Worship.   I. Title.
  BV10.2.B32   1999
264—dc21   99-21812
                                                                                CIP

21	20	19	18	17	16	15	14	13	12	11	10	9	8	7	6	5	4	3	2	1
16	15	14	13	12	11	10	09	08	07	06	05	04	03	02	01	00	99			

*To the churches who have allowed me
to lead them in worship each week:
First Baptist Church,
Clifton, Texas (1983-1986)
Valley Ranch Baptist Church,
Dallas, Texas (1986-1990)
Brookwood Baptist Church,
Birmingham, Alabama (1994-present)*

*Much of what I have learned about worship
I learned from you.
Thank you.*

CONTENTS

Prologue

WORSHIP
AS A PROBLEM

T HERE IS GOOD NEWS AND BAD NEWS ABOUT CHRISTIAN worship.

First the good news. At first glance, the state of worship today looks exciting. There is a definite revival of worship in churches throughout the world. Many Christians find themselves on a worship pilgrimage. They are coming to rethink Sunday mornings and to love corporate worship. They attend services where God meets them week after week in a dynamic and moving way. Worship has become their spiritual lifeline—they simply can't live without it!

But there is also bad news. Worship has evolved into a controversial topic for the Christian church. It even has the power to split churches. I repeat, *worship has the power to split churches!* How can this be? How is it possible that something as precious to Christians as worship could ever be the culprit in church conflicts?

Intended by God to be a foretaste of heavenly fellowship and unity among the saints, worship in today's church is too often a sore subject, a divisive issue, a hot potato that burns whoever touches it. In recent years, several distinct worship styles have emerged, with the popularity of each being attributed primarily to geographical and/or generational appeal. Megachurch leaders travel widely, extolling the values and benefits of a particular worship style that they identify as a major reason for their church's high attendance figures. Meanwhile, frustrated pastors of plateauing or declining churches try to jump-start their congregations by changing what are deeply entrenched worship styles, only to be met with what Ralph Neighbour calls the Seven Last Words of the Church: "We've never done it that way before!" For some congregations, the result is nothing less than a Worship War.

How has this happened? Why do churches so frequently argue and bicker over worship? What makes congregations split over differences in worship style?

Should we interpret the diversity of worship styles in today's church as a modern-day Babel, in which the current confusion reflects the judgment of God? Or should we see what is happening rather as a modern-day Pentecost, where God's people are praising Jesus Christ in ways and means that are not familiar to all but that are still inspired by the Spirit?

What can we do to think creatively, not defensively, about this matter? Where can a congregation turn for genuine help in understanding worship? Can anyone speak a clear word about such matters as worship styles, philosophies and trends?

This book is my attempt to help Christian leaders and congregations who are struggling with worship. I hope it will shed new light on this subject, rather than just generate more heat. I want it to become a key that will unlock this Pandora's box of confusion, without loosing even more demons into our churches. I trust that it will be a compass that will point us to the promised land of unity through praise. Above all, I want it to be a guide through the Sunday morning maze of differing worship styles. This book will fulfill its intended purpose if it helps Christians *understand* the various worship styles prevalent in our churches today and then *accept* those who worship differently.

I have written this book out of a double burden. The first burden is for pastors, ministers of music, seminarians and concerned church members. I want them to understand why worship has become such a bone of contention in so many churches. My conviction is that a clear understanding of worship styles will help to loosen the logjam that characterizes too much of the current discussion on worship. At its heart, therefore, this book seeks to identify and interpret five styles of worship prevalent in churches today.

My second burden is somewhat broader. I want to help God's people rediscover the priority and power of worship within the local church. A congregation that truly worships Almighty God, week in and week out, is fulfilling one of its primary reasons for being. As Sally Morgenthaler correctly points out, "[Worship] is the ultimate purpose of the church and has been since its beginning."[1] My hope is that this book will assist Christians in understanding the nature and importance of Christian worship so that every congregation will live up to its privilege of declaring God's absolute worth to the whole world.

As I wrote this book, several friends and fellow ministers read and commented on the ideas presented here. I especially want to offer thanks to Curtis Freeman, Timothy George, Bill O'Brien, and Fisher Humphreys and the Trinity Group for reading portions of the manuscript at its earliest stages and making helpful suggestions. Many of their "constructive criticisms" were so insightful that I chose to incorporate them. I am grateful for their interest in and commitment to this project. I also express my profound thanks to Rodney Clapp of InterVarsity Press, who believed in the value and relevance of this book from the first. His encouragement has inspired me throughout the process.

Part 1

CRUCIAL QUESTIONS

Before we begin to examine various worship
styles in depth, we need to ask and
answer three crucial questions:
What is worship?
What does worship have to do
with church growth?
What are worship styles?

One

WHAT IS WORSHIP?

HAVE YOU HEARD THE STORY ABOUT THE YOUNG BOY WHO WAS sitting with his mother in a morning worship service, bored to tears? Not much was keeping his attention, so his eyes began to roam the sanctuary, looking for something that would interest a child. Soon his gaze fixed on a bronze plaque on the wall that was covered with stars, letters and the outline of an American flag. Unaware of its meaning, he leaned over to his mother, pointed to the plaque and asked in a loud whisper, "Mom, what's that thing over there?"

She whispered back, "That's a plaque in memory of those who died in the service."

After a long pause, the little boy, wide-eyed and anxious, nudged his mother again and asked in a solemn tone of voice, "Mom, just tell me one thing—did they die in the morning or the evening service?"[1]

Have you ever felt that way? I have! Sad to say, this story was existentially true for me for many years. As a young boy growing up, I belonged to that vast army of children to whom worship means little or nothing. Unfortunately, it took a long time for me to "put childish ways behind me" (1 Cor 13:11). To be candid, I cared very little about worship throughout my childhood and teen years. Even as a young adult, I generally clocked in every Sunday morning for worship, kept my mind and spirit in autopilot and then clocked out after the final "Amen." I could identify with the anonymous worshiper who confessed, "My favorite part of worship is the closing prayer!"

What is surprising is that I grew up in a religious home. In fact, I was a pastor's kid. I attended worship services on Sunday morning, Sunday night, Wednesday evening and at revivals. But to "worship the LORD in the splendor of his holiness" (Ps 29:2) was foreign to me. I simply sat through the services, my eyes roaming the room, my mind and heart somewhere else.

At times God broke through. But most of the time I just went through the motions. In my naive mind, I thought that if I had attended a worship service, then I had worshiped God. But my inner self never embraced the spirit of heartfelt worship expressed in Psalm 95:

Come, let us sing for joy to the LORD;
    let us shout aloud to the Rock of our salvation.
Let us come before him with thanksgiving
    and extol him with music and song. . . .
Come, let us bow down in worship,
    let us kneel before the LORD our Maker;
for he is our God
    and we are the people of his pasture,
    the flock under his care. (vv. 1-2, 6-7)

Thankfully, in my midtwenties something significant happened. It all began when I took a course in seminary on Christian worship. I was so intrigued by what I read in books and heard in class that I began exploring worship at a more intimate and experiential level. I found myself asking what it really meant to declare the worth of Almighty God. I evaluated my motives for attending worship services. I started to realize the enormous distinction between merely going to church and genuinely offering praise and worship to the Lord. In Jesus' words, I was on the path to becoming one of those "true worshipers [who] will worship the Father in spirit and truth, for they are the kind of worshipers the Father seeks" (Jn 4:23). I am still on a pilgrimage. I am still making progress.

Defining Worship

As we begin our worship pilgrimage together, perhaps it will be best to try to get at the core meaning of worship. The word *worship* itself is fascinating. It is a shortened English version of the old Anglo-Saxon word *weorthscipe*, which is transliterated "worth-ship." It simply means "worthiness." Thus to worship someone means to recognize and to declare that person's worth. But to worship God pushes "worth-ship" to its ultimate limits, for true Christian worship calls us to declare the *absolute* worthiness of God and the *relative* worthiness of everyone and everything else.

One of the clearest scenes of worship in the Bible is found in Revelation 5:11-12, where John sees a heavenly vision depicting the eternal worship of Christ in heaven:

Then I looked and heard the voice of many angels, numbering thousands upon thousands, and ten thousand times ten thousand. They encircled the throne and the living creatures and the elders. In a loud voice they sang:
"Worthy is the Lamb, who was slain,

to receive power and wealth and wisdom and strength
and honor and glory and praise!"

This shows what God expects of us in Christian worship: that we
exalt the Living Lord as ultimately worthy to receive all that we have
and all that we are.

Worship is ultimately a mystery. It involves not just our own
human experience but also the very nature and character of God.
Therefore it resists a simple definition or description. Nonetheless,
a helpful way to begin to grasp its meaning is to reflect on some of
the ways in which thoughtful Christians have tried to describe it.

True worship is that exercise of the human spirit that confronts
us with the mystery and marvel of God in whose presence the
most appropriate and salutary response is adoring love.[2] (Ralph
P. Martin, author of several books on worship in the Bible)

Worship is a personal meeting with God in which we hymn,
magnify, and glorify Him for His person and actions. . . . We
worship God simply because He is God.[3] (Robert E. Webber,
professor of theology and culture at Wheaton College and
leading authority on the renewal of worship in America)

Christian worship is the glad response of Christians to the
holy, redemptive love of God made known in Jesus Christ.[4]
(Horton Davies, scholar on the history of worship)

Worship is . . .
To quicken the conscience by the holiness of God,
To feed the mind with the truth of God,
To purge the imagination by the beauty of God,
To open the heart to the love of God,
To devote the will to the purpose of God.[5] (former Anglican
archbishop William Temple)

These definitions reveal something of the majesty and marvel of Christian worship. No single sentence can begin to exhaust its meaning. It is too deep and mysterious, too broad and varied, too complex and significant to be reduced to a single statement. No article, book, dictionary or encyclopedia has been or ever will be regarded as the final word on the subject. Yet we have the opportunity of meeting the eternal and infinite God in the wonderful act of corporate worship, even if we cannot understand all that transpires in such a holy moment. What a privilege!

Worship in the Bible

For Christians, the ultimate rule of faith is the Bible. This means that we must turn to holy Scripture for our primary source of knowledge about worship. The biblical story shows us that worship is fundamentally a response of an individual or a people to a mighty act of God. The pattern that emerges in the Scriptures looks like this:

□ God powerfully acts on behalf of God's people.
□ The people respond in gratitude and praise.
□ God accepts their act of worship.

This pattern, consistent throughout the Bible, points out a central truth: in worship, God always initiates. Worship is a human response to the divine initiative. You can see the pattern in both the Old Testament and the New Testament.

Expressions of worship in the Old Testament. The history of Israel can be seen as the pilgrimage of a worshiping community. This history began when God called Abraham to be the "father of nations." With that call came divine promises of blessings such as greatness, influence, descendants and land. In response to these promises, Abraham worshiped God by building an altar (Gen 12:7-8; 13:18) and offering a sacrifice (Gen 15:1-11; 22:13-14). Abraham's call stands out as the genesis of Israelite worship.

Israel's miraculous escape from Egypt, known as the exodus, became the basis and blueprint for all future worship. God's rescue of the people from slavery constitutes the single most important event of the Old Testament. It is to the Old Testament what the cross and the resurrection are to the New Testament: the defining moment.

The exodus gave the Israelites several ways to worship God. Primary expressions included offering animal sacrifices at the Passover (Ex 12:1-28), consecrating their firstborn to the Lord (Ex 13:1-2) and singing the songs of jubilation and victory led by Moses and Miriam (Ex 15:1-21).

At Mount Sinai, God stipulated three festivals in which the Israelites were to offer worship: the Feast of Unleavened Bread, the Feast of Harvest and the Feast of Ingathering (Ex 23:14-19). This command began to instill in the people the awareness that worship involved a sacred sense of time.

After the new covenant was ratified, Moses built an altar for worship, again offered animal sacrifices, read the Book of the Covenant to the people, listened to them pledge their obedience to God and then sprinkled them with "the blood of the covenant" to confirm their commitment (Ex 24:1-8). The people were then instructed to bring offerings to God at a new sanctuary or tabernacle, which they were to build (Ex 25:1-9). This suggested that a place of worship was not only important to God but also necessary for Israel.

It fell to King David to organize the nation into a worshiping community. His first step was to bring the long-lost ark of the covenant, symbolizing the presence of God, to Jerusalem, where he had established the new monarchy (2 Sam 6). Once Jerusalem became the national center of worship, David began to plan for a marvelous temple where the people could offer their worship to God (2 Sam 7). Although he was never permitted to construct such a building, he organized the priests and Levites into ministers of temple worship and appointed them to be gatekeepers, musicians and treasurers (1 Chron 23—26). With these changes came the realization that worship required specific individuals to lead the services.

But David's most significant contribution to worship in Israel was the psalms. Many of them he wrote, inspired or commissioned. The singing of psalms, along with the rite of animal sacrifices, became the backbone of Israelite worship. The psalms, which can be understood as Hebrew poetry put to music, centered on those themes that were crucial to Israel's religion: God's mighty acts (Ps 78; 105; 106), God's kingship (Ps 93; 95; 97; 99), creation (Ps 8; 19; 33), praise and thanksgiving (Ps 30; 100; 103), confidence and trust (Ps 23; 27; 16), wisdom (Ps 1; 11; 19), lament and sorrow (Ps 42, 43, 69, 80) and Israel's kings (Ps 2; 45; 72).

But God was not always pleased with Israel's worship. When the people offered public sacrifices to God while at the same time trying to hide their secret sins, prophets arose to courageously call Israel to repentance. To the Holy One of Israel, worship could not be divorced from morality. The divine message in Isaiah is painfully clear:

> I have more than enough of burnt offerings. . . .
> I have no pleasure
>   in the blood of bulls and lambs and goats. . . .
> Stop bringing meaningless offerings!
>   Your incense is detestable to me. . . .
> When you spread out your hands in prayer,
>   I will hide my eyes from you;
> even if you offer many prayers,
>   I will not listen.
> Your hands are full of blood;
>   wash and make yourselves clean.

Take your evil deeds
  out of my sight!
Stop doing wrong,
  learn to do right! (Is 1:11-17)

Amos spoke similar words on behalf of God:

I hate, I despise your religious feasts;
  I cannot stand your assemblies.
Even though you bring me burnt offerings and grain offerings,
  I will not accept them.
Though you bring choice fellowship offerings,
  I will have no regard for them.
Away with the noise of your songs!
  I will not listen to the music of your harps.
But let justice roll on like a river,
  righteousness like a never-failing stream! (Amos 5:21-24)

As you can see, worship in ancient Israel was not static. It progressed from the primitive altars and spontaneous sacrifices made by Abraham and his kin, to the required festivals and Passover celebrations prescribed by Moses, to the elaborate tabernacle and comprehensive musical program organized by David. One final change, however, occurred when the nation suffered divine judgment for idolatry and disobedience.

Changes in intertestamental worship practices. Israel fell to Babylon in 587 B.C. The victors destroyed both the city of Jerusalem and the temple built by Solomon. Those who survived the Babylonian onslaught either remained in their homeland, now made desolate by years of siege, or were forced into exile in Babylon.

Although some of these exiles returned to Jerusalem fifty years later to rebuild the city walls and the temple, their worship was altered dramatically. Sacrifice and music gave way to the reading of the Torah, the saying of prayers and the recitation of psalms. The meaning of worship was now found in obeying the Torah. Israel had learned its lesson, perhaps too well. Since breaking the law had brought divine judgment, the people concluded that the way to avoid God's wrath in the future was to elevate the law and to strive to keep it in every way possible. Sadly, this conclusion diminished the role and importance of the sacrificial system and the musical organization that had been so integral to Israel's worship for so many years.

After the exile, the center of worship in Israel became the local synagogue, which could exist in any community where at least ten Jewish males resided. Praise marked the beginning of the synagogue service. Following the call to worship came general prayers and the recitation of the *shema:* "Hear, O Israel: The LORD our God, the LORD is one" (Deut 6.4). After these prayers came readings from the Hebrew Scriptures, followed by a sermon based on one or more of the passages read. The synagogue service effectively functioned as a bridge from Hebrew worship to Christian worship.

Worship themes in the New Testament. Although the New Testament does not prescribe a specific worship order, it nevertheless highlights several elements of worship that became very important to the earliest Christians. These first disciples worshiped by means of prayer (Acts 2:42), singing (Col 3:16), Scripture reading, preaching and teaching (1 Tim 4:13), making offerings (1 Cor 16:2), and celebrating the Lord's Supper (1 Cor 11:17-34). From a careful consideration of these New Testament worship practices, five themes emerge.

First, the purpose of worship was to glorify the God and Father of the Lord Jesus Christ. Nothing else motivated these early Christians when they gathered for worship. Their singular desire was to exalt God, that is, to celebrate the unique and supreme worth of the God who was revealed in Jesus Christ.

Second, the centrality of Christ pervades every one of the ele-

ments mentioned, whether prayer in Jesus' name, songs high-
lighting the Christ-event, preaching and teaching about the Lord
of Glory or remembering his suffering and death at the Passover
meal.

Third, the Spirit inspired each of the practices found in early
Christian worship. It was the *Paraclete* (literally "counselor," "advocate" or "one called alongside to help"—see Jn 14:16, 26) who
empowered their praying, enlivened their singing, animated their
preaching and enlightened their teaching.

Fourth, the result of worship was the edification of the church,
the people of God. You see it in the early church in Jerusalem,
where the people "devoted themselves to the apostles' teaching
and to the fellowship, to the breaking of bread and to prayer"
(Acts 2:42). You also see it in the more mature church in Ephesus,
where the Christians would "speak to one another with psalms,
hymns and spiritual songs" (Eph 5:19). In the New Testament,
worship was a primary means by which the fellowship of believers was nurtured.

Finally, congregational participation is evident in these worship
practices. All of God's people were admonished to pray, to sing, to
give, to speak to one another, to partake of the Lord's Supper. The
artificial split between clergy and laity, which later came to distin-
guish vocational ministers and priests from "ordinary" church
members, had not yet arisen. All Christians were considered the
laos, the people of God. Therefore everyone who came to worship
participated actively. In the language of team sports, there were no
benchwarmers; everyone was on the starting team.

It is obvious that both Israel and the church placed high priority
on the worship of Almighty God. Whether the admonition was
"enter his gates with thanksgiving and his courts with praise" (Ps
100:4) or "let us not give up meeting together, as some are in the
habit of doing" (Heb 10:25), the Spirit of God has always called the

people of God to render their brightest praise, their sincerest sacrifices, indeed their very lives. This, then, reveals the true heart of Christian worship: redeemed people gratefully responding to a gracious God.

Two

WHAT ABOUT CHURCH GROWTH?

Wّ HILE WORSHIP HAS EMERGED AS A HOT TOPIC IN CHURCHES in recent years, church growth has been at the center of discussion for an even longer time. Currently one of the sharpest debates in contemporary church life turns on the relationship of worship styles to church growth. In fact, in many circles the subject of worship styles is no sooner brought up than someone in the discussion mentions church growth. The questions sound like this:

"Does one particular worship style typically attract more non-Christians than another?"

"Should a church change its worship style in order to reach more unchurched people?"

"Should worship ever be considered an evangelistic tool?"

The discussions can get heated, and confusion often reigns. But there is no denying that worship and church growth are linked together in the minds of most ministers, either positively or negatively.

One of my favorite stories will bring some clarity to this subject. It's about a woman from New Mexico who was cooking breakfast for her family one morning. As was her custom, she put one tortilla after another into the skillet. In the midst of this ordinary experience, something extraordinary happened. On one of the tortillas she noticed a skillet burn. The woman said the burned tortilla looked like a face she had seen before. She kept asking herself, *Who does this look like?* Finally it dawned on her—it resembled the face of Jesus! She showed it to her husband and neighbors, and they agreed with her. Even the priest admitted the uncanny resemblance and blessed the tortilla.

The excited woman quickly enshrined the tortilla in a glass case, surrounding it with piles of cotton balls so it would look like it was floating on clouds. She then built a special altar for it and named it the Shrine of the Jesus of the Tortilla. Since truth is stranger than fiction, it comes as no surprise that over eight thousand visitors came to worship at this shrine within the next several months. And while many visitors confessed that they too saw the face of Jesus in the burned tortilla, one national news reporter said that the image looked more like ex-heavyweight boxing champion Leon Spinks![1]

Why did these people worship a flat, blackened tortilla? The answer is simple: people want to worship; they need to worship; they will worship! In 1972 Billy Graham preached in Dallas, Texas, at Explo '72, one of the defining moments of the Jesus Movement. In his sermon he said, "Whether people bow down before their God on the banks of the Nile River, the Yangtze River, the Ganges River or the Mississippi River, they all bow down for one reason: we were made to worship!"

We know that worship is one of the primary corporate acts of any local congregation. But it also provides one of the church's primary points of contact with the world. More and more, it is becoming the "front door" of the congregation, the first place where "lost" people will go, if and when they attend a church event. For this reason, it relates specifically to evangelism and to church growth and therefore needs to be considered in this context.

The church-growth movement, at its best, has refocused the attention of both ministers and laity on the priority of the Great Commission for each local congregation. When it has done this well, it has served the body of Christ as an evangelistic reminder.

At its worst, the church-growth movement has emphasized numbers, numbers, numbers to the exclusion of every other aspect of a church's life and ministry. When it has taken this one-sided approach, it has become guilty of idolatry by erecting a golden calf called "numerical growth" and demanding that God's people bow down before it!

What is needed is a well-balanced understanding of church growth that refuses to act like the video-game glutton Pac-Man and swallow up every other dimension of a church's existence. Church-growth expert Kent R. Hunter offers such an approach in an article titled "The Quality Side of Church Growth." He writes, "A study of church growth thinking leads beyond numbers to people. . . . The goal is disciples."[2] He then suggests a comprehensive growth strategy that encourages a church to grow up, grow together, grow out and grow more.

Let me revise his typology by suggesting that the four key dimensions of church growth are growing up, growing down, growing in and growing out. Consider these dimensions of growth and how each relates to worship.

Growing Up: Spiritual Maturity
Worship contributes to our spiritual maturity and "growing up" in several ways. First, it reminds us who God is, which in turn reminds

us who we are. These truths help us to counter idolatry and to nurture humility. Second, it teaches us how to pray and models prayer for us. I have learned as much about prayer by listening to Christians pray in worship as I have by reading books on prayer. Third, in worship we find the needed inspiration for ongoing spiritual recommitment. All of this contributes to our growing up spiritually.

Growing Down: Truth and Understanding

The initial accent here falls on the role of the sermon in worship. Most of us regard the sermon as an important avenue of teaching in a church. This means that the pastor is both primary teacher and resident theologian within a congregation. Biblically grounded and practically relevant sermons, in the context of worship, contribute significantly to the "growing down" dimension of church growth.

In addition, congregational singing plays the same role of teaching about God. A church member once related a personal story that confirmed the power of hymnody in the Christian life. At birth, his son was diagnosed with an extremely serious medical condition. For the next twenty-five years, this young man was in and out of hospitals, undergoing one critical surgery after another. His parents sought to trust in God to take care of their son, but they lived in uncertainty and anxiety much of the time. The father confided in me that one of the ways he sustained his faith during those dark days was to sing to himself "O God, Our Help in Ages Past" as he paced up and down hospital halls, awaiting news about the outcome of his son's latest surgery. These lyrics, proclaiming the steadfast purpose of God, renewed his faith and hope during these severe trials.

Finally, the ordinances teach us about the nature and character of God. Baptism and the Lord's Supper, when properly emphasized, lead Christians to a deeper understanding of the essential message of the gospel, which is the forgiveness of sins and the new life available in Jesus Christ.

Sermons, songs and signs all possess great potential for helping us to grow down deeply and become rooted in biblical truth.

Growing In: Fellowship and Ministry

Although Christian fellowship is fostered in many settings within the church (such as Sunday-school classes, mission teams and choirs), we should not overlook the power of corporate worship to enrich fellowship. Many of us remember growing closer to fellow church members as together we celebrated the Lord's Supper or observed a service of baptism. We have shared true Christian fellowship as we have sung, prayed and listened to a sermon. Worship contributes to a church's growth in fellowship and ministry.

Growing Out: Evangelism and Missions

There are at least two points where numerical church growth intersects worship. First, worship is a primary means by which we are spiritually formed into outward-looking persons who realize that people need the Lord. Not coincidentally, Isaiah was caught up in worshiping God when he heard the divine questions "Whom shall I send? And who will go for us?" His response, "Here am I. Send me!" grew out of an encounter with the Holy One (Is 6:8). God intends for worship to be the primary impetus for evangelism and missions. John Piper boldly states that worship is "the fuel of missions. . . . You can't commend what you don't cherish."[3]

Second, people whom we are seeking to reach for Christ and evangelize with the good news will, at some point in their spiritual journey, join us in corporate worship. Like it or not, they will probably continue to attend as long as our worship services are meaningful to them and draw them closer to God. And if we truly present our lives to God as a sacrifice of love right before their eyes, there is a good chance that they will turn to the Lord whose power and love they will feel. Sally Morgenthaler is right when she says, "Seekers can be profoundly touched by God during heartfelt, corporate worship."[4] So it is clear: worship influences evangelism and missions directly.

It is high time to call a cease-fire in the fight over whether or not worship and church growth intersect in the life of a church. We must learn to think about these two important aspects of congregational life in tandem, not apart from one another. It would be easy to separate church growth and worship artificially, pretending that the two do not relate to one another in any serious way. But both theological reflection and practical experience prove that the two are intricately interwoven. This book will attempt to show how they can be constructively related.

Two final words need to be spoken here concerning worship and church growth. First, we must refuse to regard either church growth or worship as a means to an end. Neither is the *summum bonum* (highest good) for Christians. Nothing is ultimate except God. God's first command to his covenant people was "You shall have no other gods before me" (Ex 20:3). God is more important than either worship or church growth! Second, we must actively resist the temptation to manipulate people in worship services for our own purposes, especially if those purposes are determined by a church-growth strategy. To do otherwise comes perilously close to violating God's second command: "You shall not take the Lord's name in vain" (Ex 20:7). The pastor of a Vineyard church in Canada confesses how he forgot this truth: "For the past two years I have worked to make our church a 'seeker-sensitive' congregation where visitors would feel welcome. . . . [However,] we hadn't adequately considered how we might also welcome the Holy Spirit."[5] Worship is first and foremost for God.

Is there a simple answer to how we can grow churches and at the same time worship with integrity? Surprisingly, the answer to this question is more obvious than we might expect. It is found in the answer Jesus gave when asked, "Of all the commandments, which is the most important?" He replied, " 'Love the Lord your God with all your heart and with all your soul and with all your mind and with all your strength.' The second is this: 'Love your neighbor as yourself' " (Mk 12:29-31). This formed the backbone of Jesus' ethic, and it must guide Jesus' people in their decisions and actions related to worship and church growth.

Three

WHAT ARE WORSHIP STYLES?

NOW WE MOVE SPECIFICALLY TO THE CONCEPT OF WORSHIP styles. This is a move that is distasteful for many Christians to make. Listen to the words of Lutheran pastor Peter Marty: "Pigeonholing the manner of praise is more than a disservice to God. It threatens the integrity of the body of Christ."[1] Why are some people so offended by the idea of worship styles? Because they have naively decided that all churches everywhere should worship the same way that they do! Sometimes they reason that, given the common themes mentioned earlier, every congregation should eventually reach a consensus about how to worship. That is, if every worship service in every congregation in every corner of the world contains essentially the same elements—music, prayer, the Word of God, the ordinances or sacraments, the offering—then it would seem logical that most, if not all, of those churches should worship similarly. At other times, people who hold this view simply suffer from spiritual and cultural myopia, assuming that all Christians walk, talk, look and worship the same! Marty again expresses this view when he writes, "As long as pastors and church musicians believe they must satisfy the desire of every living thing, worship is in trouble."[2]

But as past history and current experience reveal, worship has differed significantly from century to century, from tradition to tradition and from denomination to denomination. Worship is more dynamic than static, more fluid than fixed, more developmental than determinative. This is nowhere more clear than in my own denomination, the Baptists.

A Spectrum of Worship Styles

Among Baptists, worship styles can and do differ dramatically from church to church. For all who know our history and heartbeat, it is evident that Baptists have never insisted on uniformity when it comes to corporate worship. We insist on freedom not just in ecclesiology but also in doxology. As a result, we have worshiped in a variety of ways, from the revivalism of frontier missions, to the formality of big-city congregations, to the toe tapping and hand clapping of southern gospel churches, to the free and open praise style that is spreading throughout our congregations like wildfire. Baptists have never shared one common worship style in the past, nor do we now, nor will we ever.

This diversity of worship styles in my own denomination also characterizes a rapidly growing number of other Christian denominations—Methodist, Presbyterian, Lutheran, Episcopalian, even Roman Catholic. It appears that congregational worship today gives evidence of greater diversity than at any other time in Christian history.

For those who wave their Bibles and claim that Holy Scripture gives us a blueprint for worship, I have a sobering piece of news:

the New Testament nowhere endorses one specific style of worship for all believers! A careful study of the New Testament reveals that one searches in vain for a divinely sanctioned style or order of worship that all churches must follow if they are to be true churches. Rather, variety in worship styles emerged during the apostolic era and has been with us ever since.

So that this claim is not misunderstood, let me offer a word of clarification. In claiming that the New Testament never provides an express order of worship, I am not suggesting that there is no biblical guidance for corporate worship. As mentioned earlier, the Bible frequently reveals the nature and priority of worship for Israel and for the early church. The Old Testament points to the importance of sacred places marked by altars, animal sacrifices, festivals of commemoration, observance of the law, singing of psalms and the use of priests who served as ministers of temple worship. The early church continued the synagogue practices of Scripture reading, preaching, singing and prayer, and it added the Lord's Supper and baptism as well. The Bible speaks univocally and unmistakably about the value and privilege of religious worship, pointing the church in every age to constant prayer, vibrant singing, biblical exhortation, sacrificial giving, baptism as initiation and the Lord's Supper as both sign and mystery. What the New Testament *never* does is identify one particular style of worship as more Christian, more biblical or more holy than another.

Diversity in worship styles is here to stay, and no amount of wishful thinking or biblical arguing is going to change that reality! The simple fact is that not all people meet God or express thanks and praise in the same way. Therefore different churches have different styles of worship. And sometimes one church will even offer more than one style of worship.

Can these styles be identified? Absolutely! If you were to visit worship services around the United States, you would discover, amid all the diversity, several clear patterns of worship. It might be tempting to divide all these styles into the two simple categories of traditional and nontraditional or perhaps to use the three designations of traditional, contemporary and a traditional-contemporary blend. But it is becoming increasingly obvious that a more precise differentiation is necessary for a fuller understanding of these styles. I have identified five unique worship styles that are currently being used in churches in countless denominations across America and around the world. They are given here on a worship spectrum, with the left being the most traditional and the right being the least traditional.

Liturgical	Traditional	Revivalist	Praise & Worship	Seeker

Worship Styles—Gift or Blemish?

Some Christians welcome this diversity of worship styles as the work of the Spirit of God, whom they believe continually guides the church to discover new ways of worship that are faithful to the Bible. Others resent the diversity, having become convinced that the image of unity in worship has been shattered. Still others try to ignore the diversity, as though their own worship style is the only obvious and God-ordained choice. Regardless of these reactions, Christians continue to differ greatly in their approach to and practice of worship.

In my own pilgrimage, I have come to appreciate rather than despise the many worship styles operative in today's churches. This did not occur overnight, nor did it happen easily. I have been blessed to belong to several churches along the way that have exposed me to a number of different worship styles, including all five styles that I mention in this book. Most of them allowed me, even encouraged me, to "exalt the LORD our God and worship [him], for the LORD our God is holy" (Ps 99:9).

Do you need to have multiple personalities in order to appreciate worship styles other than your own? Even renowned church musician Donald Hustad describes himself as a "schizophrenic musician."[3] He freely admits that during the course of his ministry he has embraced many styles of worship and schools of sacred music, several of which appear to be incongruent with one another. But this broad experience has allowed him to be open minded and accepting toward certain types of church music that otherwise would be dismissed as being inappropriate in a particular congregation. In my judgment, Hustad is less a schizophrenic than an eclectic. He is not confused by varying musical styles. He simply appreciates the values of differing types of music.

To adopt this perspective, even grudgingly, gives greater objectivity when studying and evaluating those worship styles that differ from our own. After all, few things are more sacred to us than the way in which we learned to worship or the way we worship most effectively now. The silence of the New Testament suggests that we must be very careful before we dismiss or negatively criticize another's preferred worship style. My prayer is that this book will clarify the most significant worship styles congregations are practicing today, to the end that understanding will replace fear and that unity in diversity will be embraced as a Christian principle even in the area of worship style.

Part 2

STYLES OF WORSHIP

Now that we have thought about the meaning of
worship, the relation of worship to church
growth, and the reality and necessity of worship
styles, the time has come to examine
each of the five worship styles mentioned
in chapter three.

Four

LITURGICAL WORSHIP

L ITURGICAL WORSHIP STANDS OUT BY FAR AS THE MOST FORMAL of all the styles. With roots going deep into patristic and medieval soil, it claims the oldest heritage. This style continues to be practiced among most mainline Protestant and Roman Catholic churches, and it is gaining popularity among some evangelical congregations. In fact, in 1982 the Antiochian Orthodox Christian Archdiocese of North America, a highly liturgical denomination, received two thousand new members from evangelical backgrounds. Led by former parachurch leader Peter Gilquist, these "Campus Crusade and Billy Graham types" abandoned their independent Bible churches in order to become affiliated with the Orthodox. By way of explanation, they said that they were seeking "something more" in worship, which they hoped to find in the Orthodox liturgy.[1]

The mood of a liturgical service reflects a balance of contemplation and majesty. It places a premium on reverence. The service is well planned and completely structured. Its axiom is summarized in the quip attributed to the late John Mackay, former president of Princeton Theological Seminary: "In worship, when the choice comes down to order or ardor, I'll choose order every time."

Purpose and Biblical Models
The purpose of liturgical worship is to lead the church to bow before the transcendent glory of God, that is, to praise God's greatness and power. By comparison, the immanence or closeness of God receives much less emphasis. In this tradition, we are apt to feel God's greatness more than his nearness. We observe God from a distance, not up close.

The fullest biblical model for this style is found in Isaiah 6:1-9, where Isaiah sees a vision of the Holy God, surrounded by angels crying, "Holy, holy, holy is the LORD Almighty." The young Isaiah then confesses his sin of "unclean lips" and finds forgiveness when an angel sears his lips with a burning coal from the altar. Finally he hears the call of God, "Whom shall I send?" and obediently answers, "Here am I. Send me!" Liturgical worship seeks to follow this model in order, mood and content; the service moves from adoration to confession to absolution to commission.

The book of Psalms also contains several passages that reflect this majestic, often solemn, understanding of worship. The command in Psalm 46:10, "Be still and know that I am God," calls for a quiet sense of dignity before the Holy One. "Worship the LORD in the splendor of his holiness" (Ps 29:2) serves as a reminder that the nature and character of God are not to be taken lightly. And the summons to "bow down in worship" and to "kneel before the LORD our Maker" (Ps 95:6) suggests that being in the presence of God requires a humble spirit.

Above all, those who advocate this style of worship relish this insight and warning from the apostle Paul in 1 Corinthians 14 (although they are a little troubled that it is found in a passage where he also validates charismatic worship!): "For God is not a God of disorder but of peace. . . . Everything should be done in a fitting and orderly way" (1 Cor 14:33, 39).

Historical Precedents

Today's liturgical style accurately reflects the way many Christians worshiped in both the early church and the medieval church as well as in several branches of the Reformation church. Let's look at worship that was common to these time periods.

The early church. Following the death of the last of the original apostles of Christ, and with the close of the New Testament canon around A.D. 100, Christian worship slowly began to solidify into a more formal pattern. This pattern consisted of a twofold alternation between the sermon and the table, the service of the Word and the service of the Lord's Supper. In effect, the two emphases of the synagogue and of the upper room became fused into one service.[2]

During the fourth and fifth centuries, this set worship form solidified into even more fixed services in large cathedrals and sanctuaries. What brought about this increased order? Two factors, both related to the Constantinian Revolution, were the root causes. First, Emperor Constantine's decision to legalize Christianity as the official state religion of Rome in A.D. 313 encouraged church leaders to adopt signs of the emperor's favor, such as large, ornate buildings for houses of worship. Second, the end of state persecution of the church gave way to a previously unknown era of peace, allowing both churches and Christians the opportunity to reflect on their worship. Such reflection contributed to a set, planned, precise order of service. The liturgical style of worship was firmly in place, and it would stay this way for centuries.

The medieval church. The millennium that stretched from A.D. 500 to A.D. 1500 witnessed several significant developments in the worship of the church. First, a noticeable split developed between clergy and laity. The people of God were no longer one, but two. Only the clergy were permitted to read Scripture, pray in services and touch the elements of the Mass. The laity were relegated to being mere passive observers in worship. We call this undue emphasis on the role of the clergy in the life of the church *sacerdotalism* (from the Latin root *sacerdos,* meaning "priest"). It succeeded in keeping rank-and-file Christians from pouring their hearts into worship. The liturgical style took on a distant mood. The transcendent God revealed himself only to religious professionals.

Second, the Mass eventually developed into a mechanical ritual rather than a spiritual observance. The Lord's Supper became not only the centerpiece of medieval worship but also the primary means of both granting and withholding grace. This exalted view of the Eucharist, and of other rites within the church, is called *sacramentalism.* It succeeded in reducing a sacred mystery to a lifeless liturgy.

Third, worship became more important than the worshiper. Style superseded the Spirit. The aim of worship was to present a flawless reenactment of the drama of Christ's death in the Eucharist. Lost in the process was the goal of ordering a service so that *all* of the believers present would sense the blessed presence of Christ in every aspect of worship. This exaggerated emphasis on the outward dimension of religion is called *formalism.* It succeeded in hardening the forms of worship until all spontaneity of the Spirit was crowded out.

Given these developments, you can see why the church, and especially its worship, was ripe for reform. Three glaring deficiencies stood out. First, God had become unapproachable. Priests repeated the Mass and read the Bible in Latin. The laity had little or no participatory role in Christian worship. They simply could not approach the God of the church.

Second, Christ's death had become unintelligible. The mystery of the "unbloody sacrifice" confused the average believer. Transubstantiation, the doctrine that the wafer and the wine literally became the body and blood of Christ when consecrated, provided clergy with topics for discussion and debate. But it was seldom more than an abstract and meaningless theory to the laity. The idea of earning merits through good deeds, as taught by the priesthood, robbed the atonement of any meaning or joy. The centerpiece of the gospel—the death of Christ for the salvation of the world—had been perverted into a commercial doctrine that would have been unrecognizable to the apostles.

Finally, the Spirit's power had become unavailable. No one was teaching that "to each one the manifestation of the Spirit is given for the common good" (1 Cor 12:7). To the contrary, clergy acted as if they were omnigifted. The Spirit had little or no freedom to elevate prayers, embolden preaching or inspire singing. The entire system of the church's worship had systematically eliminated any room for the Spirit of God to work.

To its credit, the church in the Middle Ages did manage to maintain a sense of wonder and mystery in worship. But the negative dynamics described above far outweighed this lone benefit. For better and for worse, the medieval Roman Catholic service is part of the legacy of the liturgical style.

The Reformation church. With the advent of the sixteenth century came massive reform within the church. The Protestant Reformation had many faces, but at its heart was the desire to replace corrupt medieval worship practices with a more biblically centered pattern. Both Martin Luther and Thomas Cranmer criticized and corrected prevailing Roman worship. They sought to liberate liturgical worship from rote and superstition.

The Protestant Reformer who most changed worship was Martin Luther (1483-1546). In *The Babylonian Captivity of the Church,* he attacked the entire sacramental system of the fourteenth and fifteenth centuries. Luther's desire was to put the sacraments in their place by subordinating them to the Word of God in worship.

His objections to the sacramental theology of his day can be summarized as follows. First, he rejected the idea that the seven sacraments of the church originated with Christ. Instead, he argued, only baptism and the Lord's Supper came directly from the teachings of Jesus. This refocused worship on the gospel.

Second, Luther claimed that the sacraments require human faith to work. They are not operative by themselves. He rejected the Roman teaching of *ex opere operato* (grace comes "through the performance of the work" of the priest). He claimed that faith is necessary for the sacraments to be effective. In doing so, he elevated the role of the unschooled but faithful worshiper.

Third, he believed that the Mass needed liberating from three "captivities" by the medieval church: the Lord's cup was kept from the laity and was reserved for the clergy only; the doctrine of transubstantiation went beyond biblical teaching in its explanation of what happened to the bread and wine at the table (Luther preferred to speak of Christ's bodily presence at the Mass in a unique, special way); and the Mass was seen as a human offering *to* God, somewhat akin to bribery, rather than an offering *of* Jesus Christ, the God-man. Once liberated from these repressive teachings, the Lord's Supper could begin to assume its proper meaning in worship.

Fourth, Luther decried the fact that baptism was held captive to the false teaching of salvation by works. He insisted that salvation was by grace alone through faith alone. Again, this call for faith in God restored a proper emphasis on divine grace.

Finally, he objected that the church was also holding the doctrine and practice of penance captive to a theology of works. That is, he objected to the common practice of "paying" for penance with earthly riches, in the hope of buying one's way to heaven. By insisting that access to heaven had already been purchased by Christ's atonement, he was calling necessary attention to the power of the cross.

Luther did more, however, than offer a scathing critique of medieval worship. He also put forth several reforms that he hoped would correct the abuses listed above. He began by elevating the laity to equal rank with the clergy. He emphasized the priesthood of all believers, with the corollary that all worshipers were priests before God. To accommodate this view, he argued that prayers should be said, and most music written and sung, in the common language of the worshipers. He also moved Mass from an annual observance to a weekly observance. Finally, he demanded that the Word of God should be preached at every service of worship, so that the only captivity within the church would be the people's captivity to Holy Scripture. Luther's correctives sought to bring warmth and life out of cold, dead services. The liturgical style showed itself capable of being vibrant.

The Church of England. Liturgical styles of worship continued to develop in other parts of Europe. The Protestant Reformation had a right wing, which could be found in England, where King Henry VIII broke with the Roman Catholic Church in the early sixteenth century. While Luther and others sought church reform for spiritual reasons, Henry did so for a more mundane reason: he wanted to divorce his wife, Catherine of Aragon, who was unable to bear him a male successor, in order to marry Anne Boleyn! When Pope Julius II refused to annul the marriage, Henry severed England's formal ties with the Roman Catholic Church, declared himself political head of the Church of England and named Thomas Cranmer as archbishop of Canterbury, the spiritual head of the church.

Cranmer's impact on worship style is difficult to overestimate. He set the course for the future of Anglican worship when he compiled the Book of Common Prayer in 1549 and required all churches in the land to use it as a guide for worship. It has been called "the most important single event in the reformation of the worship of English-speaking people."[3] Written in the vernacular of the people, it allowed everyone who attended services to participate actively. Cranmer instituted daily worship services, known as the daily office, throughout England. Staple items in these brief services were public prayer and the systematic reading of Scripture.

Liturgical worship had found new language and new life. Forever associated with it in the future would be the Lord's Supper, the primacy of Scripture and set prayers from the Prayer Book.

Current Expression

What does liturgical worship look, sound and feel like today? Let's consider a service that is typical of this style.

Music. The minister of music or the organist/choirmaster leads the congregation in singing three hymns, all sung from the hymnal. These hymns generally fall under the classification of traditional or classic hymns, as opposed to gospel hymns. They focus on the adoration of God, the life of the church and the duties of discipleship.

Hymns of praise and adoration are objective in nature. They highlight the greatness and glory of God, not the worshiper's thoughts or feelings about God. Examples of such hymns for a liturgical service include

☐ "Come, Thou Almighty King"

☐ "All Creatures of Our God and King"

☐ "Praise to the Lord, the Almighty"

☐ "Praise the Lord! Ye Heavens, Adore Him"

☐ "O Worship the King"

☐ "Joyful, Joyful, We Adore Thee"

Hymns concerning the life and ministry of the *ekklesia* focus on the objective identity and mission of the church. The worshiper's response is generally not as important as the hymn's theological truth. Among the most popular of this genre of hymns about the church are

☐ "The Church's One Foundation"

☐ "In Christ There Is No East or West"

☐ "Lead On, O King Eternal"

☐ "God of Grace and God of Glory"

Hymns that focus upon the daily demands of Christian discipleship stress service over testimony and social concern over evangelism. Favorite hymns for the Christian life include

☐ "Dear Lord and Father of Mankind"

☐ "Be Thou My Vision"

☐ "Take My Life and Let It Be"

☐ "We Are Called to Be God's People"

Charles Wesley and Isaac Watts contributed many of the hymns that are frequently used in liturgical services.

The choir provides most of the special music in liturgical services. Its repertoire consists mostly of anthems composed by older classical composers such as Bach, Mozart or Handel; anthems by modern classical composers such as Ralph Vaughan Williams; and traditional modern anthems such as those by Gordon Young. The occasional soloist chooses pieces from the classical tradition as well.

The pipe organ reigns supreme as the primary musical instrument in liturgical churches. Seldom is a piano used, because it is viewed as more of a solo instrument. Taped musical accompaniment is usually out of the question.

Scripture reading. The reading of Holy Scripture occupies a prominent place in the service. The corporate confession of sin often incorporates Scripture passages, and the call to worship and the benediction do the same. In addition, at least two other public readings from the Bible occur, usually an Old Testament reading and a New Testament reading. The psalms are frequently read at numerous points during the service. The Common Lectionary[4] generally dictates the choice of Scriptures for the day.

Offering. Reverent fanfare accompanies the collection of the offering. The minister often blesses the offering as it is presented by the ushers at the front of the sanctuary. The congregation may sing the doxology as a response of gratitude.

Sermon. When the pastor stands to preach, the sermon likely will follow the Christian year, revolving around the great themes of Advent, Lent, Easter and Pentecost. The lectionary will guide the pastor to preach "the whole counsel of God" over a three-year period. The sermon tends to have a more intellectual than emotional approach and a more social than evangelistic appeal. Following the sermon is a period of commitment, often tied to a closing hymn of dedication or service. Altar calls are foreign to the liturgical service.

Sacraments and ordinances. The congregation celebrates the sacraments or ordinances frequently, with the Lord's Supper being served weekly in most mainline denominations and monthly in congregations coming out of the Free Church movement (see chapter five). This pattern differs greatly from the Zwinglian and Anabaptist tendency to offer Communion only quarterly. Baptism is usually celebrated less frequently.

Other elements. In some liturgical services, the congregation recites in unison the Lord's Prayer. In many, the people sing the Gloria Patri. In most, they repeat the Apostles' Creed as a common confession of faith.

Order of service. How are all of these elements usually arranged in a liturgical service? The order of service below, drawn from Proper 8 of Year C in the Revised Common Lectionary, follows typical liturgical style.

The Service of the Worship of God
The Twelfth Sunday After Pentecost
Organ Voluntary: "In Thee Is Gladness" (Bach)
Choral Introit: "Jesus, Stand Among Us" (Filitz)
Call to Worship
MINISTER: Worship the Lord in the beauty of holiness.
CONGREGATION: It is a good thing to sing and make music to your name, O Most High.
MINISTER: The Lord inhabits the praises of his people.
CONGREGATION: Great is the Lord and greatly to be praised! His greatness is beyond understanding!
MINISTER: O come, let us sing unto the Lord. Let us bow down before the Lord, our Maker.
Hymn of Praise: "Joyful, Joyful, We Adore Thee" (HYMN TO JOY)
Invocation
Psalter Lesson: Psalm 77:1-2, 11-20
Prayer of Confession
Declaration of Pardon
Old Testament Lesson: 2 Kings 2:1-2, 6-14
Anthem: "Psalm 121" (Millard Walker)
Pastoral Prayer and Lord's Prayer
Gospel Lesson: Luke 9:51-62
Offertory Hymn: "Take My Life and Let It Be" (HENDON)
Offertory Sentence and Prayer
Offertory: "Praise to the Lord, the Almighty" (WALTHER)
Presentation of Tithes and Offerings
Doxology (Old Hundredth)
New Testament Lesson: Galatians 5:1, 13-25
Sermon: "Love and the Spirit of Freedom"
Holy Communion
Hymn of Commitment: "O Master, Let Me Walk with Thee" (MARYTON)
Benediction
Organ Postlude: "Psalm XVII" (MARCELLO)

Church Growth

I spent ten years of my childhood and youth worshiping in a liturgical service at First Baptist Church of Richmond, Virginia. The pastor preached in cutaway tails and pronounced the Aaronic blessing ("The Lord bless you and keep you...") at the end of the service. The minister of music directed the choir (with his head) as he simultaneously played the organ, which was hidden behind the chancel. Every Sunday morning we sang the doxology and the Gloria Patri and said the Lord's Prayer in unison. We celebrated the Lord's Supper monthly. This was my introduction to the Baptist version of liturgical worship. The mainline Protestant version differs in only a few particulars, the most obvious being the frequency of Holy Communion.

To some people, church growth and liturgical worship are incompatible. They believe that the two subjects do not even belong in the same discussion. Nevertheless, liturgical worship thrives in many growing churches on Sunday mornings.

Dynamic liturgical worship exists at St. Luke's Episcopal Church in Birmingham, Alabama, a congregation that has experienced sustained growth for over a decade. Rector John Claypool said that this style appeals to people because, in the language of philosopher Søren Kierkegaard, church attenders have grown tired of being the audience that merely watches the preacher-actor, who is supposedly being prompted by God. Instead people yearn for the chance to be the actors in worship, performing before God who is the true audience, with the preacher serving as prompter. Claypool also thinks that people want their whole bodies to participate in worship rather than simply listening with their minds. He thinks liturgical worship meets these needs.

Claypool further believes that there is drawing power in the Eucharist as a means of grace in addition to preaching. He even calls the Eucharist a "spiritual transfusion." This movement between the meaning of the pulpit and the mystery of the altar enriches worship.

Finally, he believes that the stark contrast between liturgical worship and the world's entertainment mindset has contributed to the renewed interest in the ancient liturgy.

Evaluation

Strengths. The liturgical service of worship suggests several strong points. First, its form and structure point the congregation to God, who is worthy to be praised in majesty and honor. In a day where God is being trivialized and marginalized by a consumer-oriented church, any reminder of God's glorious nature is welcome.

Second, magnifying God's transcendence evokes in the worshiper a sense of awe. God is called the Holy One of Israel throughout the Old Testament. The angels in heaven worship God by crying out day and night, "Holy, holy, holy is the Lord God Almighty" (Rev 4:8). Therefore it is only right that we "tremble before him" because "he is to feared above all gods" (Ps 96:9, 4).

Third, the prominence of Scripture reading, the centrality of the Lord's Supper and the pattern of the Christian year reveal a deep reverence for the Word of God. Interestingly, Scripture saturates the liturgical service more than it does any other worship style.

All of these dimensions of the liturgical style can make for dynamic worship that is deep, rich and profound.

Warnings. This style of worship is not without its critics, however. For some Christians, the God who is worshiped in the liturgical service seems unapproachable, more the Wholly Other than the Good Shepherd, more like Aristotle's Unmoved Mover than like the God and Father of our Lord Jesus Christ. Majesty can overshadow mercy. Grandeur can overpower grace. As Marva Dawn points out, "Holiness without love incites terror. . . . Worship that focuses on God's transcendence without God's immanence becomes austere and inaccessible."[5]

For others, the form and structure of the liturgy do not provide a vehicle for effective worship but actually impede worship. The liturgy prohibits spontaneous responses of praise. It also quenches any sovereign surprises from the Spirit. For them, the form of the liturgical service quickly degenerates into dead formalism, nothing more than religion by rote.

Finally, the cerebral dimension of the service may sacrifice the emotional appeal or the evangelistic emphasis that some Christians want and expect. Objectivity seems to be valued far more than subjectivity. The service appeals more to the head than to the heart.

My personal perspective. I, for one, love good liturgical worship. The bells and candles, set prayers and readings provide me with a sense of awe that I find almost nowhere else in our culture. Confronting my sin and Christ's sacrifice weekly in the Lord's Supper keeps me lashed to the cross. Repeating the same actions over and over do not necessarily anesthetize me to the Spirit's touch. I almost always meet God in these services.

But I fear that this style has a limited future in North America. It has so little point of contact with most of the younger generations that its days may be numbered. As we enter a postmodern, post-Christendom world, I predict that more and more churches will cast aside liturgical worship as a vestige of "older days and older ways" and never pause to appreciate its beauty and value.

The liturgical style appeals to all Christians who believe that the goal of worship is to bow before the holiness of God in structured reverence. At its best, it fills the worshiper with a profound sense of the majesty of God. It points the believer to the grandeur and glory of God. At its worst, it conceals the love and grace of the gospel. And it can too easily snuff out the Spirit's fire by refusing to relinquish control of the service.

Five

TRADITIONAL
WORSHIP

ALTHOUGH DECIDEDLY LESS FORMAL THAN THE LITURGICAL style, traditional worship still follows a planned and structured order. While its ministers describe the service as nonliturgical, it would be more accurate to identify this style as semiliturgical. One minister of music has described it as "informal dignity." It originated when liturgical worship moved across the Appalachian mountains, and it earned a permanent place in Protestant worship when that new frontier became settled. As such, the traditional style is a hybrid of liturgical worship and frontier revivalism (see chapter six).

Purpose and Biblical Models
Gratitude and preaching dominate traditional worship, suggesting that its overall purpose is to lead the congregation to thank God for his goodness and to hear God speak through his Word.

The primary biblical model seems to be the Ephesian-Colossian "style" that stressed Christ's teaching and congregational singing. This pattern, which emerged in the first-century church, finds expression in Colossians 3:16, where Paul tells his readers, "Let the word of Christ dwell in you richly as you teach and admonish one another with all wisdom, and as you sing psalms, hymns and spiritual songs with gratitude in your hearts to God." (See also Eph 5:19-20.)

Historical Precedents

What we are calling traditional worship began to appear soon after the Middle Ages ended. It was a modification of medieval worship, intended to correct its abuses.

The Reformation. Worship during the Protestant Reformation included more than the liturgical approach alone. A modified liturgical style appeared in both Switzerland and England during the sixteenth and seventeenth centuries. These services, less structured than those fashioned by Luther and Cranmer, were the forerunners of our modern-day traditional worship.

John Calvin (1509-1564) was the leading Reformer in Geneva, where he served as both pastor and city leader. He judged harshly the prevailing worship practices in the Roman Catholic Church. Listen to his scalding words:

Instead of the ministry of the Word, a perverse government compounded of rules lies there, which partly extinguishes the true light, partly chokes it. The foulest sacrilege has been introduced in place of the Lord's Supper. The worship of God has been deformed by a diverse and unbearable mass of superstitions.[1]

His suggested reforms for worship proved to be more thorough than those of Luther and Cranmer. He tolerated less Roman influence than did the other two reformers. Consider these worship changes he proposed.

First, Calvin saw the Lord's Supper as a tool of church discipline, not as an elaborate ritual. He stressed the need for worshipers to enter into an intense period of self-examination before partaking of the elements, in order to be purified of all sins. The Lord's Supper was offered monthly or quarterly, but not weekly (although Calvin himself preferred weekly observance). This reform made the Lord's Supper not only more accessible to the masses but also more personal for the individual.

Second, Calvin held that Mass was a sign of God's grace and that it had to be received in faith in order to be effective. He believed that Christ was truly present in the Mass, but in a spiritual way only. By removing all vestiges of superstition, he encouraged the widespread practice of faith in the power of the gospel.

Third, Calvin demanded that music in worship conform to three norms: Psalms, not hymns, were to be sung; the melody, not harmonious parts, was to be sung; and organs were to be played in one's home, not in a worship service. Although these regulations look harsh to us now, their original purpose was twofold: to simplify worship so that everyone could participate actively and to center worship in the Word of God, instead of in formalities or superstitions.

Finally, Calvin required that the weekly service include exegetical preaching, which sought to explain and apply a particular passage of Scripture. This reform would insure that every worshiper was confronted every week with the promises and demands of God. In this way only could heartfelt worship occur.

Free Church traditions. Another lively tradition that sprang up in the seventeenth century is known as the Free Church, so named because of its love of freedom—freedom to return to New Testament patterns of worship, freedom from state interference in matters of worship and freedom from other churches in determining the elements and order of worship. Although this movement began on the European continent with the Anabaptists, several significant expressions later emerged in England. Two of these conformed to the style that we today call traditional worship.

The earliest groups identified with the Free Church were the Separatists and the Puritans.[2] They sought to reform worship within the Anglican Church by holding up the Bible as the sole liturgical criterion. That is, they tried to apply one of the Reformation cries of a century earlier, *sola Scriptura,* to the theology and practice of worship. They demanded that every worship practice have a clear biblical precedent.

They also argued that worship matters ought to be settled within each congregation, where the members know the issues best, rather than at a national level, where those least familiar with the situation would make the decision. Their goal of "local relevance" became an implicit second authority for determining worship. Out of these principles emerged two hallmarks of Free Church worship: spontaneous, informal prayers and practical, applicable sermons.

The Separatists, more radical than the Puritans, were a heterogeneous group composed of Baptists, Independents, Presbyterians and Congregationalists. They wanted to reform the Church of England as quickly as possible. If they were unable to effect change as rapidly as they expected, then they were prepared to separate. What drove the Separatist movement was the desire for "pure" congregations (not contaminated by Anglican traditions) to come together to worship and celebrate the Lord's Supper.

One of the most famous Separatist pastors was John Robinson, who led his congregation of Pilgrims to the Netherlands, where they found sanctuary from religious persecution in England. Out of this group came a determined little band of Separatists who sought even more religious freedom. In 1620 they returned to England, boarded the *Mayflower* and sailed to Plymouth, Massachusetts, where they founded a colony in New England. Two other important Separatists who preceded Robinson were John Smyth and Thomas Helwys, who moved from Anglicanism to Puritanism to Separatism before Helwys finally founded the first Baptist church on English soil in 1612.

Puritanism refers to another heterogeneous group of dissenting Anglicans, most of whom were Calvinists. During the reign of Queen Mary (a devout Roman Catholic) in England between 1553 and 1558, Protestant Reformers there were routinely banned to Europe. After Mary's death, they returned to their homeland, bringing with them the Calvinist, Genevan, anti-Roman reforms that they had adopted while they were in exile.

The Puritans objected to Anglican worship on several counts. First, they thought that the vestments worn by priests at Mass looked popish and betrayed an unholy alliance with the Roman Catholic Church. Second, they rejected other Roman practices such as the use of water, kneeling for Communion and the admission of papists to Communion. Third, they banished the traditional fixed, printed order of worship, as well as fixed prayers. In other words, they argued against any element of worship that had no scriptural warrant! As a result, what often remained were nothing more than long prayers and long sermons.

Although different from one another in many ways, Separatists and Puritans had one thing in common: they both thought Cranmer's reforms, instituted in the Book of Common Prayer, did not go far enough. They wanted to complete the English Reformation.

Under the long arm of Calvin and his successors, liturgical worship was transmuted into a less formal, more open style. Out of this ferment came a pattern of worship that is recognizable and powerful in today's church: traditional worship.

Current Expression

What does traditional worship look like today? Consider these major elements of worship.

Music. The minister of music leads the congregation in the singing of four or five hymns. Although contemporary Christian songs and praise choruses are beginning to find their way into some traditional services, hymns remain the staple for congregational music. Favorite hymns of praise for traditional services are

- ☐ "Holy, Holy, Holy!"
- ☐ "To God Be the Glory"
- ☐ "Praise Him, Praise Him"
- ☐ "We Have Heard the Joyful Sound"

These hymns have gained prominence because they give equal emphasis to both the transcendence and the immanence of God. They highlight both God's greatness and God's goodness. At the same time, they balance the objectivity of God's nature and the subjectivity of the one who is worshiping.

In America, traditional worship reflects its revivalistic background in its love for gospel hymns. However, they are not the brand of gospel hymns that tend toward crass sentimentalism or that might be called maudlin. They emphasize the salvation of the believer but avoid emotional manipulation. The best-loved hymns of the gospel genre include

- ☐ "Amazing Grace"
- ☐ "Blessed Assurance"
- ☐ "The Solid Rock"
- ☐ "Leaning on the Everlasting Arms"
- ☐ "Love Lifted Me"

Hymn writers who figure prominently in the gospel hymns used in traditional worship are Philip Bliss, Fanny Crosby, B. B. McKinney and Isaac Watts.

Soloists and ensembles augment the choir in the traditional service, usually singing two pieces per service. The choir regularly sings traditional modern anthems, hymn arrangements by musicians like John Ness Beck, contemporary anthems such as those by Tom Fettke and Mark Hayes, and occasional contemporary popular Christian music arrangements by Michael W. Smith and others. Soloists and ensembles sing primarily hymn arrangements, contemporary Christian music or gospel music. Classical pieces appear in the music repertoire occasionally but are often limited to seasonal holidays.

The organ and the piano join forces as the primary musical instruments in the traditional service. The organ may be pipe or electronic, and the piano is usually a grand or a baby grand. In larger churches, an orchestra of strings, woodwinds, horns and percussion enlarges the sound. Interestingly, the electronic synthesizer has started to make an appearance as well, usually to replicate orchestral sounds. Churches that practice traditional worship may use taped musical accompaniment, but not all do so.

Scripture reading. There is usually one Scripture reading in a worship service. It takes one of two forms: a responsive reading from the hymnal or a solo reading directly from the Bible.

Offering. The offering is received prior to the sermon or prior to the special music that precedes the sermon. Recently a number of churches have moved the offering to the end of the service, after the sermon, indicating its responsive nature.

Sermon. The pastor's sermon derives from a specific Scripture passage, chosen in one of several ways. It may be selected according to the Christian year, the denominational year, the civic calendar or a personal preaching plan. The message may be expository or topical, but it will generally appeal to both heart and head. Following the sermon, the pastor issues a public invitation for people in the congregation to make a commitment to Christ and to the church during the singing of the final hymn.

Ordinances. Believers in traditional churches celebrate the Lord's Supper weekly, monthly or quarterly, depending on tradition. Baptism may be observed more frequently than in liturgical services.

Order of service. A traditional service, centered around the theme of joy, could easily take the following form.

Organ Prelude: "Great Is Thy Faithfulness" (arr. Harris)
Choral Call to Worship: "Praise Ye the Name of the Lord" (Young)
Hymn of Praise: "Rejoice, Ye Pure in Heart" (MARION)
Invocation and Welcome
Responsive Reading: Matthew 7:7-11
Solo: "I Asked the Lord" (Peterson)
Pastoral Prayer
Offertory Hymn: "We're Marching to Zion" (MARCHING TO ZION)
Offertory Prayer
Offertory: "Come All Christians, Be Committed" (Hayes)
Anthem: "Open Thou Mine Eyes" (Harlan)
Sermon: "Whatever Happened to Joy?" (Gal 5:22-23)
Hymn of Commitment: "The Master Hath Come" (ASH GROVE)
Benediction
Organ Postlude: "Toccata in C" (BACH)

Church Growth

As a young boy, I attended the Gaston Avenue Baptist Church in Dallas, Texas, a large, thriving congregation where my father was pastor. It typified the traditional style that has been the mainstay of much evangelical Protestant worship fare. When we gathered on Sunday mornings, we sang not only great hymns of the church but also gospel hymns. We heard a Scripture passage read by one of the ministers, or we participated in a responsive reading from the back of the hymnal. The choir sang an anthem, and the minister of music sang a solo. The sermon came straight from the Bible. This is traditional Christian worship at its best.

Traditional worship is alive and well at many churches, including Dawson Memorial Baptist Church in Birmingham, Alabama. Gary Fenton, pastor at Dawson, reflected on church growth in his congregation: "For a traditional service to grow, the worship tradition needs to reflect what people in the church's target area believe and feel about God. That is, this style reaches people from a traditional religious culture, who grew up being familiar with religious language." He also stated that "the people attracted to a traditional service have a high need for structure and have usually tasted success through following the system." Dawson's traditional worship style continues to attract new people every week.

Philip Wise, pastor at First Baptist Church in Dothan, Alabama, added these insights: "This style can have great appeal in the Bible belt, where worship historically has been traditional. Traditional worship is sophisticated and refined and orderly and appeals to white-collar, educated people who will not be comfortable at either a fundamentalist or a charismatic church."

As is evident, traditional worship and church growth can and frequently do go hand in hand.

Evaluation

Strengths. The strengths of the traditional service are somewhat predictable. In many ways, it allows for the best of both worlds in worship. Transcendence and immanence, objectivity and subjectivity, intellect and emotions—these are all balanced fairly evenly. The service is formal enough to maintain dignity yet informal enough to warm hearts. It is structured enough to point to God, yet it is more relaxed than the liturgical style. The God worshiped in this service is both great and good, holy and helpful, awesome and approachable.

Warnings. As expected, however, the traditional style has its detractors. For those who long for a richer liturgy, the lack of Scripture readings in the traditional service proves offensive, as does the less frequent observance of the Lord's Supper. Many think the traditional style offers "milk without meat," a watered-down version of "pure" worship, a concession to modernity.

At the same time, the structure that is present prevents more participatory worshipers from making the spontaneous responses that well up within them and seek less structured expression. To put it bluntly, these Christians fear that the traditional service has become "lukewarm—neither hot nor cold" (Rev 3:16).

My personal perspective. Traditional worship holds a special place in my heart. Sentimentally, I treasure it because it is the way I first learned to worship. It was the very first style I "tried on." In many ways, it still fits. I continue to appreciate its informal dignity as well as its twin emphases on gratitude and preaching.

But I am hesitant to embrace traditional worship, with no modifications, as the dominant style of the future. I have two critical concerns. First, while numerous older Christians cannot imagine a better way to worship, most younger believers think this style has become too stilted and predictable. In America, entering a sanctuary where traditional worship is going on can feel like taking a trip back in time to the 1950s. Although many will still prefer its routine rhythms, new generations of disciples will likely desire a new worship style that reflects a new day. Therefore, to flourish in the future, the traditional style must be blended with more contemporary elements of worship.

Second, the world of the twenty-first century will not be as compartmentalized as it was in the mid-twentieth century. This means that worship in the twenty-first century will not be as compartmentalized either. Services can no longer simply alternate between hymn, prayer, Scripture reading and sermon, with each element standing alone, seemingly unrelated to the rest of the service. (I recently heard a British Christian refer to the tendency to insert a hymn between other elements of worship as "the hymn sandwich.") To flourish in the future, the traditional style must be streamlined into an organic whole, so that the worshipers find themselves carried along, through a seamless service, into the very presence of the God who delights in their worship.

Traditional worship offers believers a warm yet structured way to offer praise to God. Seeking to include enough reverence to avoid tackiness and enough informality to avoid staleness, this style continues to appeal to many Christians. At its best, it provides a *via media* for those who do not like either liturgical worship or more contemporary worship. At its worst, it simply provides a temporarily safe harbor for those who refuse to face the radical changes that have occurred in our culture over the last half-century.

Six

REVIVALIST WORSHIP

Today's revivalist worship patterns itself after the tradition developed on the American frontier at the beginning of the nineteenth century. Characterized by informality, exuberance, zeal and aggresive preaching, this style of worship seeks to turn lost sinners toward a merciful God. The upbeat mood of the service directly impacts the emotions, so that people will "feel" God's presence during worship. Although revivalist worship prides itself in being antiliturgical, the order of service is still generally planned and structured.

Purpose and Biblical Models

In a revivalist service, the primary purpose is evangelistic: to reach the lost with the gospel of Jesus Christ. Peter's preaching at Pentecost as recorded in Acts 2 best exemplifies the biblical model for this style of worship. When Peter proclaimed the kerygma in Jerusalem that day, three thousand Jews believed the gospel and were baptized. Those in the revivalist tradition believe that this should still be the goal for Christian worship: to reach as many unbelievers as possible with the good news about Christ.

Another favorite Scripture passage that has shaped this worship style is Paul's charge to Timothy, a young pastor who was his son in the faith: "Preach the Word; be prepared in season and out of season; correct, rebuke and encourage" (2 Tim 4:2). This suggests a secondary purpose of revivalist worship—to motivate believers to live godly lives in an ungodly world and to share their witness with unbelievers.

Historical Precedents

Revivalism dislikes and distrusts most outward "forms" of worship that reflect liturgical or traditional theology and values. Its adherents resist or reject whatever smacks of formality or formalism. They want nothing in the service but "the simple gospel" preached unapologetically (and generally loudly!).

The revivalist tradition has surfaced in Christian history many times since the Reformation. You find it wherever you find a desire to simplify worship and a suspicion of external signs and forms. This pattern first emerged clearly in the worship reforms instituted by Ulrich Zwingli, George Fox and John Wesley. The revivalist style became institutionalized in American frontier worship.

Ulrich Zwingli. Ulrich Zwingli (1484-1531) was a Protestant preacher in Zurich who is best remembered for his tragic decision in 1529 to break with Luther over the meaning of Mass and especially over the words of institution ("This is my body. . . . This is my blood"). Behind Zwingli's celebrated decision lay the belief that God is pure, transcendent Spirit and the conviction that the physical world is unable to convey spiritual reality to humans. As a result, he purged worship services in Zurich of every physical sign, including images, music and musical instruments. He even destroyed pipe organs whenever he found them in sanctuaries and cathedrals!

Because he believed that Jesus meant "this represents my body" and "this represents my blood," Zwingli regarded Mass as a mere symbol. He thought that Jesus was not present in a more special way during the Mass than at other times. Although he allowed Mass to be offered only quarterly, he required daily preaching services in Zurich.

Quakers. Quakerism, or the Society of Friends, is another expression of the Free Church movement in England. Founded by George Fox (1624-1691), it was the most radical of all reforming attempts. Fox and his followers rejected all clergy, service books, visible sacraments, preaching, choirs and organs. With no "outward forms," their services retained nothing but silence and occasional shared reflection. This allowed them to reach their ultimate goal of worshiping God according to inner spiritual promptings (the "inner light"), waiting on God in quietness. This shows what happens when *all* external signs in worship are rejected.

Methodists. A final expression of Free Churches is Methodism, founded by John Wesley (1703-1791) and Charles Wesley (1707-1788). Some historians believe that Methodism was not a true Free Church expression because it was too closely tied to Anglicanism. After all, both Wesley brothers died as ordained priests in the Church of England. At the very least, however, Methodism was a countercultural movement within the Anglican Church, emphasizing enthusiastic worship marked by robust singing and biblical preaching, often done by laypeople. Small-group worship experiences, weekly Communion and the necessity of conversion became Common themes of this reforming movement within Anglicanism, which eventually became a church of its own. When Methodism reached America, its preachers became known as "circuit riders" because they traveled by horseback from town to town, preaching evangelistic sermons and planting new churches.

Frontier worship. "The most prevalent worship tradition in American Protestantism (and maybe in American Christianity)" has been dubbed the "frontier tradition" or the "revival tradition."[1] It refers to those religious groups that grew and thrived on the American frontier west of the Appalachian Mountains in the eighteenth century. They included, among others, the Baptists, Methodists, Disciples of Christ and Churches of Christ.

Because of their independent spirit, these settlers generally held little interest in an organized, hierarchical church structure. And because they were typically uneducated or illiterate, they had no use for either trained clergy or prayer books. As a result, they developed their own distinct brand of churches with their own distinct style of worship.

Their theology sprang out of a handful of core commitments: simple Biblicism, local church autonomy and pragmatism. Their worship services were characterized by evangelistic preaching to the lost, congregational singing based on revival themes and freedom from all unnecessary tradition. Their camp meetings had a threefold pattern: the song service, the sermon and the invitation or "harvest" of converts.

The frontier-church experience radically changed the way many American Christians worshiped and viewed worship. Nineteenth-century American frontier worship bore little resemblance to any style or form of worship described in the Old or New Testament or practiced during the church's first eighteen hundred years. The purpose of worship was no longer to worship a holy God but to evangelize sinful humans. In the past, worship had been designed for Christians. It had emphasized the preaching of the Word, the celebration of the Mass or both. Now it had become a tool for evangelism. "Baptism and the Lord's Supper took a back seat to the supreme 'sacrament' of the sermon. . . . Worship became a means to an end rather than an end in itself."[2]

Current Expression

Revivalism is an American creation that has many historical precedents. In today's church it often looks like this.

Music. Congregational singing assumes great importance in this style of worship, for music stirs the emotions and prepares the heart for the sermon. The congregation, under the leadership of a minister of music or a song leader, sings four or five hymns with great gusto. Although some of these are contemporary Christian songs or praise choruses, most are gospel hymns. Depending on the church, these hymns might be "classic" gospel hymns from a standard hymnal, or they could be southern-gospel songs from a Stamps Baxter songbook.

Favorite gospel hymns in revivalist services center on at least four themes: revival, conversion, prayer and heaven. First are hymns of revival and renewal, stressing the need for God to visit his people in power, such as

☐ "Lord, Send a Revival"
☐ "Revive Us Again"
☐ "Send a Great Revival"
☐ "There Shall Be Showers of Blessing"

Second are gospel hymns that highlight conversion:

☐ "Victory in Jesus"
☐ "Nothing But the Blood"
☐ "Just As I Am"
☐ "The Old Rugged Cross"

Third are hymns that inspire prayer:

☐ "In the Garden"
☐ "Near to the Heart of God"

☐ "Tell It to Jesus"

☐ "What a Friend We Have in Jesus"

Finally, there are hymns like the following that describe life in heaven:

☐ "When We All Get to Heaven"

☐ "Shall We Gather at the River?"

☐ "O That Will Be Glory"

☐ "When the Roll Is Called Up Yonder"

Fanny Crosby, B. B. McKinney and Ira Sankey could be called the patron saints of revivalist music.

Special music by the choir, an ensemble or a soloist inspires the congregation. Two or three special music pieces are offered at each worship service. The choir never sings classical music. Instead it sings gospel-music arrangements, such as those by John W. Peterson; peppy hymn arrangements, like the ones by Camp Kirkland; and contemporary anthems. Soloists likewise never sing classical music. They prefer gospel pieces and contemporary Christian songs. Taped accompaniment is used regularly in the majority of these churches.

The piano and organ provide musical accompaniment. The piano functions both as a solo instrument and as a primary means of accompaniment. The organ may be either a Hammond organ or a newer electronic organ, but it would rarely be a pipe organ. Pipe organs are too often associated with liturgical worship to fit a revivalist service.

Scripture reading and offering. Scripture passages are seldom read in revivalist worship services, except at the time of the sermon. The offering is received midway through the service, often during the special music that precedes the sermon.

Sermon. When the pastor enters the pulpit to preach, everyone in the congregation knows that the sermon is the main event for the day. Even though music is important in the revivalist service, the "song service" is often considered to be little more than the preliminary that warms up the worshipers for the preaching. As one pastor put it, "The music sets 'em up so the sermon can knock 'em out!" The congregation can generally count on hearing an evangelistic message calling everyone present to "get saved." The preacher willingly accepts Paul's call to "do the work of an evangelist" (2 Tim 4:5).

Even if the sermon text is not evangelistic, the pastor will move to a gospel theme and an evangelistic appeal. Following the admonition often attributed to Charles H. Spurgeon, the revivalist preacher "makes a beeline for the cross" in every sermon. By design, the message focuses on an explanation of sin and redemption, with the aim of "harvesting" unbelievers in the worship service, that is, leading them to make a personal decision to follow Jesus Christ.

The public invitation that follows the sermon is often lengthy in order to allow non-Christians to recognize their need of Christ. These altar calls can last ten minutes or longer.

Ordinances. The Lord's Supper receives little attention in revivalist churches. They tend to set the Lord's table no more than three or four times a year and seldom if ever on Sunday mornings. Because of the evangelistic emphasis, however, baptism is observed much more frequently, sometimes weekly.

Order of service. A revivalist service centers on the theme of confronting Jesus Christ, especially his death on the cross. A representative service looks like this.

Piano Prelude: "Revive Us Again"
Hymn: "Victory in Jesus"
Hymn: "There Shall Be Showers of Blessing"
Prayer
Welcome and Announcements
Solo: "In Heaven's Eyes"
Testimony: Deacon of the Week

Hymn: "Saved, Saved"
Offertory Prayer
Offertory: "In the Garden"
Special Music: "Tell It to Jesus" (KIRKLAND)
Sermon: "Fire from Heaven" (Lk 9:54)
Invitation Hymn: "At Calvary"
Closing Chorus: "We Are One in the Bond of Love"

Church Growth
Two of the best examples of well-known revivalist churches in the Baptist tradition are North Phoenix Baptist Church (during the 1970s and 1980s, when Richard Jackson was pastor) and First Baptist Church of Jacksonville, Florida. This style is the modern heir to the frontier revival service. The music and sermon both focus, sometimes almost exclusively, on Christ's death and on God's offer of salvation to all who believe. Extended invitations provide ample time for an attender to be convicted of sin and to be converted to Christ. Both churches have experienced strong numerical growth over the years.

Evaluation
Strengths. The revivalist style of worship has some clear strengths. Its informal attitude and exuberant mood invite the participation of worshipers. In fact, it is virtually impossible to sit still during a revivalist service! The music, both congregational and special, excites human emotions. The sermons challenge the will. Above all, this type of service places high priority on the new birth—a new relationship to God through Jesus Christ.

Warnings. At the same time, however, revivalist services have some glaring deficiencies. Because this style so emphasizes evangelism in worship, the net result is often an imbalanced worship service. The congregation's need to worship God is overlooked or not taken seriously.

Once the purpose of worship is defined in terms of reaching the lost with the gospel rather than of worshiping God, several consequences follow. First, the church family receives a steady diet of "milk" and not "meat," of evangelism and not instruction, of kerygma and not didache. Second, the canon for sermons becomes relatively small, since the majority of messages are supposed to be evangelistic. Third, the canon of hymns becomes equally limited, for the same reason. Fourth, the constant preaching about conversion to believers often leads to their rebaptism. Christians begin to think that the only way to please God is to be saved and baptized, even if they have already done so before.

For those who believe that worship has no other end than to glorify God for his nature and his acts, the revivalist style raises additional concerns. First, the music tends toward emotionalism. Second, the sermon can stress judgment and condemnation over grace and forgiveness. Third, the invitation can become manipulative. In short, worship can become a means to an end, which offends those who appreciate the vision of worship as expressed by the late Franklin M. Segler, longtime professor of pastoral ministries at Southwestern Baptist Theological Seminary. "Worship is an end in itself; it is not a means to something else," Segler wrote. "We worship God purely for the sake of worshiping God."[3] William H. Willimon, dean of the chapel at Duke University, is even more pointed:

> In its most basic sense worship has no other function than the joyful, ecstatic abandon that comes when we meet and are met by God. Any attempt to use worship to educate, manipulate, or titillate can be a serious perversion of worship. . . . God is not to be used for our own purposes, not even for our own good purposes.[4]

My personal perspective. While I like the excitement and zeal of a revivalist service, it seldom brings me face to face with the living God. The constant attention to non-Christians can get old if you are already a Christian. A real, live, honest-to-goodness revivalist service makes me feel like I'm back on the frontier in a premodern world. I believe that this style had its heyday in the nineteenth century and will not return to glory in the future.

Revivalism magnifies God's offer of salvation in Jesus Christ to everyone who will believe. The nagging question is how to wed evangelistic appeal and the praise of God, how to join together gospel invitation with God-centered worship. At its best, the revivalist style shows that this can be a feasible marriage. At its worst, it proves that it has always been an unholy union.

Seven

PRAISE & WORSHIP

ONCE LOOSELY AND PEJORATIVELY IDENTIFIED AS "PENTECOS-tal worship," the style now popularly known as contemporary or "praise and worship" describes an upbeat, loud, informal service in which the congregation actively seeks the immediate presence of God. Worshipers celebrate their experience of God through outwardly expressive, sometimes uninhibited, acts of praise. This style often includes overt charismatic tendencies such as speaking in tongues, interpreting tongues and exorcising demons. But this style of service is not always "charismatic."

Some evangelicals who participate in praise and worship services identify themselves as noncharismatic. They still believe that worship should involve the whole body, so they love to clap their hands, raise their arms, sway to music and shout out loud. But they are not comfortable publicly practicing what they consider to be the spectacular or "sign" gifts. A friend of mine calls this *charismatic-light:* "hands, no tongues!"

Purpose and Biblical Models

The purpose of a praise and worship service is to guide the congregation to offer a sacrifice of praise to the Lord in a spirit of joyful adoration. The Old Testament model that inspires this style of worship is Psalm 150, where the people of God are invited to praise the Lord "with the trumpet, . . . with the harp and lyre, . . . with tambourine and dancing, . . . with the strings and flute, . . . with the clash of cymbals." In the New Testament, this style first emerged in Corinth around A.D. 50, where believers incorporated miracles, prophecy and glossolalia (speaking in tongues) into their worship (1 Cor 12—14).

Other Bible passages have influenced and legitimized this approach. One psalmist commands: "Clap your hands, . . . shout to God with cries of joy" (Ps 47:1). Another psalmist exclaims: "I will praise you as long as I live, and in your name I will lift up my hands" (Ps 63:4). Paul reiterates this sentiment when he writes, "I want men everywhere to lift up holy hands in prayer" (1 Tim 2:8). Scripture certainly testifies to the validity of the style we are calling praise and worship.

Historical Precedents

We will now look at the two most profound expressions of this style to be found in American history: black worship and Pentecostal worship.

Black worship.[1] The genesis of black worship in America may be found in that dark and murky period of the country's history when white Europeans and Americans brought black Africans, against their will, to the "New World" to be slaves. Despite the horrors and injustices of slavery, many of these Africans came to faith in Jesus

Christ, whom their captors and masters preached. As new Christians, they gathered together for corporate worship. What emerged was a new chapter in the history of American worship, born out of the travail of the African-American experience of forced captivity and labor.

For over three and a half centuries, black worship has existed as a dynamic and powerful reality within the larger Christian church. As we will see, beneath all of its distinctive features is one overriding reality: these are Christian brothers and sisters "whose understanding of God in Jesus the Christ is uniquely contextualized in suffering and struggle."[2] In other words, the key that unlocks the meaning of black worship is the oppressive experience of slavery.

The first characteristic common to black worship is a love for preaching that addresses God's Word to those social structures that may mistreat or marginalize African-Americans. The sermons of the late Reverend Martin Luther King Jr., packed with powerful prophetic quotations from the Old Testament and spiced with appeals to love and forgiveness from the New Testament, provide an excellent example of the boldness and beauty of black preaching.

A second characteristic is the lively and spontaneous response of worshipers to the sermon while it is being preached. Verbal agreement with a sermon point may take the form of phrases such as "Yes, Lord," "Preach it, brother," "Well, well" or "Amen!" These external responses, animated and inspired, spring from an internal hunger for the promises of the Word of God to find fulfillment quickly, so that skin color and national heritage will no longer be the basis for inequity and discrimination.

A third distinctive of black worship is the power and prevalence of music. The "Negro spiritual," as it was once called, exposed the suffering hearts of "African people in America," who, having been forcibly brought to "a strange and alien land," found themselves "enslaved, marginalized, denied respect, and oppressed by the very people who introduced them to Christianity."[3] But out of ashes came beauty. Black spirituals, with their plaintive melodies and pleading words, reveal a sensitivity to the Spirit of God that is often absent from traditional hymns and contemporary choruses.

Black gospel music today often reflects its African roots in the use of drums and other rhythm instruments. It also encourages and elicits from the congregation such responses as raising their arms, clapping their hands, closing their eyes and swaying their bodies. Black worship music is not so much performed or observed as it is lived, felt and experienced. This points to Melva Wilson Costen's claim that the "genius of Black worship is its openness to the creative power of God that frees and enables people, regardless of denomination, to 'turn themselves loose' and celebrate God's act in Jesus Christ."[4]

Heartfelt prayer is a fourth characteristic of black worship. When African-Americans enter into prayer in a service of worship, they truly obey the command of the psalmist to "pour out your hearts" to God (Ps 62:8). Addressed to any and all of the "three persons" of the Godhead, these prayers express thanksgiving, confess sins and especially ask for divine power to live like Christ in the midst of persecution and injustice.

A final feature to be noted is the length of the service. When African-Americans gather for worship, often the clock does not dictate how long they meet. The only rule to follow is this: worship until you have finished! As a result it is not unusual for services to last two hours, sometimes even longer. Longings for liberty and cries for freedom simply cannot be confined to a one-hour service!

Common to all black worship is the dominant note of hope. Against all odds, African-Americans have survived legalized slavery and institutionalized segregation. The richness of their worship points to a stubborn belief that the God whom they worship will, one day, lead them into the promised land where they "are no longer foreigners and aliens, but fellow citizens with God's people" (Eph 2:19) and where Christians, regardless of race, are "all one in Christ Jesus" (Gal 3:28).

Pentecostal worship. The most recent wide-scale development in American Protestant worship is Pentecostalism, a distinctively twentieth-century phenomenon. Historically, Pentecostalism is usually traced back to the extended revival that occurred in Los Angeles in 1906 at the Apostolic Faith Gospel Mission on Azusa Street. William Seymour, a holiness preacher who was conducting services there, stressed the need for a second baptism of the Spirit, which he identified with speaking in tongues. Out of that revival has grown a massive worldwide movement of charismatic worship that has affected, if not transformed, virtually every Christian denomination.

Worship among Pentecostal and charismatic Christians has several distinctive features. First, it is more unstructured than structured. Following the "leading of the Spirit," worship leaders reject formalism and embrace spontaneity in both the content and the sequence of worship. Christians who identify with the mainline Protestant denominations or with many of the Free Churches feel uncomfortable in Pentecostal worship services for many reasons, one of which is that the service seems to have neither rhyme nor reason. But to the Pentecostal, this is simply one of the happy consequences of doing what the Spirit says.

Second, Pentecostalism places a high premium on "body life," that is, the full participation of all members of the body of Christ in worship. The entire congregation is invited to participate by exercising their spiritual gifts. Whoever feels led is free to speak in tongues, interpret tongues, prophesy, heal, cast out demons or perform an ecstatic dance or song. Such charismatic activity is one of the hallmarks of Pentecostal worship.

Third, the goal of the service is for every worshiper to have an immediate experience of the Spirit. Consequently, the Bible often receives remarkably little attention. It is seldom read or quoted in context, and preaching often fails to be rooted and grounded in Scripture. The result is that the Spirit's presence is frequently sought apart from the written revelation of God. This tendency to separate Spirit from Word has invited many criticisms of Pentecostal theology and worship, most notably the charge of hypersubjectivism.

Culturally, Pentecostalism has traditionally appealed primarily to people of lower socioeconomic level. This reality is seen throughout the varieties of Pentecostal churches, including those affiliated with the United Pentecostals, the Assemblies of God, the Church of God in Christ, the Church of God (Cleveland, Tennessee), the International Church of the Foursquare Gospel, independent charismatic churches and denominational charismatic churches.

Current Expressions
Not all praise and worship services are charismatic or Pentecostal. Many simply utilize more recent musical styles in order to adore God in the language of younger and more contemporary worshipers. But either way, today's praise and worship services are vivacious, dynamic and packed with energy. They contain the following elements of worship.

Music. Music is what makes this service so upbeat. The congregation sings a lot, usually eight to ten songs in the course of the service. Sometimes they sing a medley of several songs in a row, repeating the stanzas over and over. Although some congregations still use hymnals, more are printing the words to the songs in the bulletin or displaying the lyrics on the wall by means of overhead projector. This allows worshipers to look up rather than down while they are singing. The minister of music typically leads congregational singing, although praise teams composed of several singers are being used more and more for this purpose.

Praise and worship congregations sometimes sing traditional or gospel hymns, but more often than not they "sing to the LORD a new song" (Ps 96:1). This means they sing praise choruses such as "Glorify Thy Name" and "I Love You, Lord"; contemporary Christian songs like "Majesty" and "Shine, Jesus, Shine"; and Scripture songs such as "Thou Art Worthy," "As the Deer" and "We Bring the Sacrifice of Praise." The lyrics tend to be more subjective than objective, more devotional than doctrinal, more affective than cognitive.

For more traditional Christians, this new music may sound unfamiliar. Its roots are not in the Reformation or the Great Awakening or even the American frontier. It is not the music of Isaac Watts, Charles Wesley or Fanny Crosby. This music grew out of the Jesus Movement, a spiritual revival among teenagers and young adults in America during the late 1960s and early 1970s. Songs that were written, performed and recorded by young people active in the Jesus Movement began to appear in church services across the country by the mid-1970s. Those songs, and their modern-day offspring, provide praise and worship churches with a vast repertoire of congregational music. Songs produced on the Maranatha, Hosanna/Integrity and Vineyard labels are among the most popular songs for this style of worship.

The choir or praise team usually sings one or more pieces of special music. Rather than singing classical or modern anthems, they sing hymn arrangements and contemporary anthems like those by Mark Hayes and contemporary popular Christian music arrangements by Bruce Greer and others. Soloists follow the same pattern, singing the contemporary Christian music of Amy Grant, Steve Green, Twila Paris or any other popular artist. Taped musical accompaniment is a regular feature for these services.

Musical accompaniment is usually some combination of piano, electronic organ and digital synthesizer. Backup bands, with guitars and drums, are becoming standard for these services as well. The sound approaches that of light rock-and-roll or soft popular music, thus appealing to a younger generation of Christians who may not like classical music and do not identify with revivalism.

Scripture reading and offering. While these services do not offer a steady diet of Scripture readings, they still provide for a Bible passage to be read. Tithes and offerings may be received in the middle of the service or at the very end, but regardless of the time, the congregation perceives the offering as an important act of worship.

Sermon. In charismatic praise and worship services, the sermon often begins with a passage of Scripture and then quickly moves to challenge the congregation to live the "victorious Christian life" through exercising sign gifts such as healing, exorcism and speaking in tongues. The public invitation then calls for people to be delivered from demonic oppression and to receive spiritual, emotional and physical healing.

In noncharismatic services, the pastor frequently preaches practical sermons from the Bible, applying a biblical text to the demands of modern life. Sermons tend to fall into one of two categories. They may emphasize matters of daily Christian discipleship, such as prayer, obedience, spiritual gifts and spiritual warfare. Or they may resemble the Christian self-help approach often identified with Robert Schuller. In that case they will deal with biblical perspectives on such matters as stress, happiness or addiction. The invitation that follows the message challenges believers to recommit their lives to the lordship of Jesus Christ, expressed in obedient daily living.

Ordinances. The Lord's Supper is celebrated quarterly, monthly or even weekly if the congregation is a charismatic Episcopal or Catholic church. Baptism usually is celebrated frequently, although the observance may be relegated to Sunday-evening worship services.

Order of service. While a praise and worship service is decidedly nonliturgical, the ministers often plan the service so that it follows a clear structure and order. Such a service, when planned around the theme of following Jesus, would resemble the following model.

Prelude: "Majesty"
Songs for the Outer Court
"Lord, I Lift Your Name on High"
"How Majestic Is Your Name"
"We Bring a Sacrifice of Praise"
"Be Exalted, O God"
"I Love You, Lord"
Prayer
Welcome and Invitation to Praise
Praise Team: "I've Just Seen Jesus"
Songs for the Inner Court
"Shout to the Lord"
"Thou Art Worthy"
"Glorify Thy Name"
"Emmanuel"
"In My Life, Lord, Be Glorified"
Songs for the Holy of Holies
"Abba Father"
"Cover Me"
"As the Deer"
Solo: "God and God Alone"
Sermon: "Following Jesus" (Lk 9:57-62)
Time of Commitment
"Sanctuary"
"Lord, You Are"
"Lord I Will"
Offertory Prayer
Offertory: "Freely, Freely"
Closing Chorus: "We Will Glorify"

Church Growth

A significant example of a church that practices the praise and worship style is the Church at Brook Hills in Birmingham, Alabama. Rick Ousley, pastor, explained the church's philosophy in these words: "The priority of our fellowship is to worship—and this encompasses music, prayer, preaching and everything else done in the service."

He explained the appeal of his church's worship services to those who attend or join, saying, "In the Bible belt, many people are dysfunctional churchpeople. They were raised in church, had a childhood faith but never adapted it to adulthood. A contemporary worship style attracts them because it is more like modern life (especially the sermon topics and the music style) than their earlier memories of church."

He described the services at Brook Hills as "relaxed, redemptive, contemporary and celebrative." The Church at Brook Hills has experienced phenomenal growth since it was started in 1990. This should come as no surprise, for most students of church growth identify praise and worship as the style most compatible with rapid numerical growth in a congregation.

Evaluation

Strengths. The praise and worship style is a relative newcomer to Protestants and evangelicals, having once been regarded as in the exclusive domain of black worship or Pentecostalism. Nevertheless, it has developed quite a following among Christians in the church today. Its strengths revolve around three constants: a celebrational mood, a sense of intimacy with God and active participation. First, the service overflows with excitement and joy. Fueled by the worshipers' expectations and the upbeat music, the praise and worship style celebrates the presence of a tender heavenly Father, a victorious Lord Jesus Christ and a powerful Holy Spirit. Second, worshipers experience an intimate encounter with God. They sense a deep awareness of his presence through the spiritual and emotional impact of the music, prayers, testimony and sermon. Finally, this style allows great freedom to respond to the perceived movement of God's Spirit, whether by singing with raised hands, praying with outstretched arms, clapping as an expression of affirmation or saying "amen" during the sermon. Such participation causes the congregation to believe that they are participating in the dialogue and drama of worship and truly worshiping God in the Spirit, a privilege that they do not ever want to give up.

Warnings. There are some blind spots in the praise and worship style, however. First, because experience plays such a prominent role, some Christians feel that these services shortchange theology. With the obvious emphasis on emotional response, this style is sometimes accused of providing entertainment or of degenerating into a religious pep rally.

Second, Christians from traditional churches often regard the choruses as doctrinally shallow and musically simplistic, not to mention redundant. The very nature of "contemporary" Christian music insures that many of the songs used are quickly dated. An unhealthy dependence of this style of worship on Christian music's Top 40 list is a common criticism mentioned by its detractors.

Third, some onlookers fear that the subjectivity and freedom within the service are nothing more than organized chaos. To their chagrin, gone are the order and structure that characterize most of the other styles mentioned thus far.

My personal perspective. Over the past decade, I have become an avid supporter of the praise and worship style. I like the upbeat music and the intimate feeling of the service. I appreciate finding God's nearness so easily. I am frequently moved to spiritual intimacy and tears in such services. Along with more scholarly researchers,[5]

I think that this will be the dominant form of worship in the foreseeable future.

I must confess that I am still unconvinced of the need for sign gifts in worship, especially when they are practiced with emotional excess. Yet I rejoice that the Third Wave of charismatic church life has changed the face of worship in America and around the world. I think the change is for the better.

The fastest-growing churches in the world today are found in the Pentecostal and charismatic traditions, which practice the praise and worship style. At its best this style reflects the freedom of the Spirit that is the birthright of every believer and that leads to greater intimacy with God. At its worst this worship style degenerates into mindless emotionalism, where "zeal is not based on knowledge" (Rom 10:2).

Eight

SEEKER
SERVICE

A RELATIVELY NEW ADDITION TO SUNDAY MORNINGS IS THE
seeker service, a style that depends more on one or two specific
persons than do the other styles. The concept of a seeker service
achieved popular recognition in the late 1980s when Bill Hybels,
pastor of Willow Creek Community Church in suburban
Chicago, received the attention of the national press in several
magazines and newspapers. Having originated and practiced this
unique, nontraditional style for a decade, Hybels began to
promote it at a "pastors' conference" sponsored several times a
year by his church. At these conferences, he explained why and
how he initiated a seeker service and how any pastor could do
the same. As a result, pastors have flocked to these conferences
to learn the nuts and bolts of planning and leading a seeker
service. These factors account for the rising popularity of this

style of service, especially among the younger generation.

Many people also identify Rick Warren, pastor of Saddleback Valley Community Church in Mission Viejo, California, with the seeker model. Warren, however, does not practice a true seeker service as Hybels does. Saddleback's approach to worship is a creative, California-style blend of the seeker service and the praise and worship style. This reveals the difference between Willow Creek's "seeker-driven" service, where every aspect of the service focuses on communicating the gospel to lost people, and Saddleback's "seeker-sensitive" service, in which the goal is to lead Christians to worship God without the "cultural baggage" of traditional language and forms.[1]

Actually, we might be most accurate to call Robert Schuller the father of the seeker movement. Although best known for his translation of Christian doctrines into culturally familiar concepts (such as equating *faith* with *optimism*), Schuller really pioneered the seeker-service idea throughout his ministry at the Crystal Cathedral in southern California. I once heard him say at a pastors' conference, "My goal every Sunday morning is preevangelism." That summarizes the seeker service perfectly.

Purpose and Biblical Models

If some of this terminology sounds foreign to the uninitiated, then a simple definition will clear things up. A seeker service is a toned-down, upbeat evangelistic service for "seekers," that is, for non-Christians who are seeking God but who have not yet made a personal commitment to Christ. It is *not* a service of worship designed for Christians. Rather, its purpose is to present and explain the gospel in nonreligious terms and in nontraditional ways to unbelievers. Seekers are given the best time to meet (Sunday morning), their own music to hear (in contemporary style) and answers to their deepest questions ("felt needs").

Church members are expected to bring their non-Christian

friends to these services, which are specifically designed to communicate the Christian message in ways that do not threaten or scare off unbelievers. In other words, the "target audience" of a seeker service is non-Christians. The informal attitude and nonliturgical style may conceal the fact that the service has been carefully planned and structured by the ministers, perhaps more so than any of the other four styles.

The biblical model that guides the seeker style is the story of Paul's preaching about an "unknown god" in Athens, as recorded in Acts 17:16-34. The passage relates how Paul accommodated the presentation of his message to his hearers in order to get its content across to them. Cultural accommodation, without gospel compromise, is the goal of the seeker service.

Current Expression
Music. Believing that seekers do not want to sing many congregational songs and cannot yet worship God, the minister of music or the praise team leads the congregation in singing only one praise chorus or Scripture song during the service, such as "Lord, I Lift Your Name on High," "This Is the Day" or "How Majestic Is Your Name." The words to the song are projected onto the wall by means of an overhead projector.

The praise team or soloists perform the special music, singing almost exclusively contemporary Christian music like that recorded by Twila Paris and Steven Curtis Chapman. The "feel" of the musical presentation is similar to a concert by a popular Christian singer.

A piano, a digital synthesizer and usually a rock or jazz band accompany both congregational and special music. Taped accompaniment also is widely accepted in seeker services where "live" instruments are not possible.

Scripture reading. When a Scripture reading is included in the service, as it often is, the reader carefully, often humorously, explains the background and meaning of the passage in a planned introduction. Behind this practice is the desire and intent to make the biblical message intelligible to those who do not understand religious terminology.

Offering. In some seeker services an offering is collected, while in others it is not. In those churches where the offering is a regular part of the seeker service, it usually takes place at the end. The minister explains that guests are not expected to contribute to the offering, other than to drop a visitor's card in the plate if they have chosen to complete one.

Sermon. Many seeker services have implemented dramatic presentations, which attempt to introduce the topic of the sermon in a form that is readily acceptable to unchurched persons who live in an age of television, cinema and theater. The actors and actresses in these dramas do not dress in bathrobes and reenact a Bible story. They wear clothes just like those worn by people in the congregation that day, and they present humorous and poignant theme interpretations that resemble television sitcoms and dramatic episodes, though these are obviously abbreviated for the sake of time. Drama communicates a story to the "television generation."

After the drama has raised a pertinent question, the minister preaches a sermon that addresses the "felt needs" of modern life from a Christian perspective. Rather than give expository sermons, the pastor usually preaches topical messages that are preevangelistic in nature. They are designed to challenge seekers to consider seriously and thoughtfully the value and importance of Jesus Christ for their lives. A public invitation is not extended every week but only occasionally to "draw the net" for those seekers who have decided to become believers.

Ordinances. Neither baptism nor the Lord's Supper is celebrated in the seeker service, because it is admittedly not a worship service for Christians.

Order of service. The elements of a seeker service follow a logical flow, as seen in the following mock service built around the theme of learning about Jesus.

Band Warm-up: "Strength of My Life"
Praise Song: "Holy Ground"
Solo: "The Great Adventure"
Scripture Reading: Luke 9:57-62
Drama: "Ordinary Christians"
Announcements
Prayer
Offertory: "Step by Step"
Solo: "Casual Christian"
Message: "What It Takes to Be a Christian"
Closing Prayer

Since the seeker service, by design, focuses on unbelievers and not on Christians, there is usually a true worship service, often called simply the "believers' service," offered on either Sunday night or Wednesday night for church members. It generally reflects the praise and worship style already described. This is the setting in which the ordinances are celebrated.

Church Growth
The seeker-service movement claims astounding numerical church growth. Consider the two most well-known expressions in the United States. Willow Creek Community Church currently attracts fifteen thousand people to its three seeker-driven services every weekend (one on Saturday evening and two on Sunday morning). Pastor Hybels is considered the patron saint of the seeker-service movement.

Saddleback Valley Community Church presently draws ten to twelve thousand worshipers to its seeker-sensitive services every Sunday. Pastor Warren is an avid proponent of culturally relevant worship services. The impact of these two churches and their pastors on contemporary worship is so deep and widespread that it cannot be measured. Pastors from many denominational and non-denominational churches attend conferences led by these two church-growth practitioners and then try to lead their churches to implement the concept of a seeker service. As a result, seeker services are popping up all over the country.

In my observation, however, few "pure" seeker churches exist anywhere. Not many are truly seeker-driven or seeker-directed, where the entire service is structured for seekers only. Most congregations that are experimenting with or seriously attempting this style are offering a seeker-sensitive or seeker-oriented service. That is, the worship services are planned in such a way that seekers will not be turned off by the "cultural baggage" of traditional Christianity.

One example of a seeker-sensitive church is McCart Meadows Church in Fort Worth, Texas, where Lee Johnson is pastor. According to Johnson, "Before every service we ask the question 'How would this relate to newcomers?' This question is asked about every item of worship." Such is the norm for a church with a seeker-friendly service.

Evaluation

Strengths. As long as one remembers Hybels's forthright and constant reminder that the seeker service is not a true worship service for Christians to praise and glorify God, it is not hard to recognize several strengths of this style. First, its aim is to reach unbelievers, who are "without hope and without God in the world" (Eph 2:12). The sensitivity of the seeker service to the culture in which non-Christians live reveals a deep commitment to build bridges for the gospel into the world of unbelievers. It is a practical attempt to reproduce the approach of the apostle Paul to people who are separated from Christ: "I have become all things to all men so that by all possible means I might save some. I do all this for the sake of the gospel" (1 Cor 9:22-23).

Second, the Bible is treated as relevant to modern life, not as a relic of antiquity. From Scripture readings to dramatic presentations to sermons, the Bible presents practical answers to the problems that unbelievers face in this world.

Finally, when the seeker service is devoted solely to evangelism, a separate service can be devoted to "true" worship. But this twofold approach to weekly worship also creates more than its share of problems.

Warnings. The proponents of the seeker service need to reflect upon some dangerous blind spots. First, there is the constant criticism that "packaging" the gospel so that unbelievers can understand it may lead to compromising the message. A similar charge is that the overt use of entertainment features in order to attract non-Christians may result in the commercialization of the church, the marketing of the gospel, the watering-down of Christian worship and the manipulation of evangelism.

Hybels, Warren and their disciples seek to be faithful to the apostolic example of cultural accommodation without gospel compromise. But serious questions will always hang over the heads of those who advocate this style: Does this new medium in any way change the old message? If so, should medium adjust to message or should message adjust to medium? And if message is trimmed to suit medium, then by what standard will one judge the content of the message? Pastors and church leaders who plan seeker services will have to be diligent and careful to seek first the kingdom of God (Mt 6:33) lest they fall into the age-old tendency of trying to please those who seek not the gospel but only "what their itching ears want to hear" (2 Tim 4:3).

A second warning addresses the tendency for congregations to move their regular worship service to another day of the week in order to offer a seeker service on Sunday morning. Many question whether it is wise to change the time of congregational worship from the Lord's Day, the day on which believers have met since the time of the apostolic church, to another day—regardless of the justification offered. The question may be framed like this: Should Sunday be the day for Christians to gather in worship, in recognition both of Jesus' resurrection on the first day of the week and of the universal practice of the Christian church ever since then? Or is one day as good as any other for worship, in recognition of Jesus' statement that "the Sabbath was made for man, not man for the Sabbath" (Mk 2:27)?

Third, others who are fully committed to the church's task of evangelism believe that the seeker style has substituted a "come and hear" approach to evangelism for the "go and tell" approach of the Great Commission.

My personal perspective. My experiences with seeker services have all been positive. I even led one church I pastored to offer a seeker-sensitive service. The results were impressive: unchurched people and marginalized Christians immediately began attending. And such is the testimony of numerous churches who are offering seeker services. A worship service that adopts a more "user-friendly" approach, yet refuses to apologize for its core convictions, will consistently reach those who have given up on God, or on the church or on Christianity. I think this approach will deeply influence worship expressions in the early twenty-first century.

The emphasis on seekers as described here is relatively new in American Christianity. But it is sweeping the church by storm. At its best, the seeker service functions as a modern-day, updated evangelistic service, striving for a somewhat subtle presentation of the "narrow road" of Christianity. At its worst, it is the gospel without teeth.

Part 3

IMPORTANT ISSUES

Assuming that these five basic worship
styles make sense, we now turn from
understanding worship styles to implementing
them. This last task before us will call
us to deal with three practical, nitty-gritty
matters related to our theme: choosing a worship
style, including all of the worship elements
in a service and preparing for worship.

Nine

CHOOSING A WORSHIP STYLE

IF YOU SAT IN ON A CHURCH SERVICE AT ANY CHURCH IN AMERICA this Sunday, you would observe a congregation at one of three points in relationship to its worship style.

Many of these congregations are happy and content with their worship style and are totally uninterested in exploring other options. The great majority of their members like the prevalent worship style, find themselves spiritually enriched by it and believe that there is no good reason to change it.

Other churches, however, are facing crucial decisions about whether or not to modify their style or adopt a new style altogether. Whether the stated reason is to accommodate the diverse worship interests of current members or to reach new members, this challenge will continue to become more and more common.

Still others have recently gone through emotionally wrenching experiences caused by an unwanted alteration of worship style. One story I know about firsthand concerns a church that for years had happily enjoyed a liturgical-traditional worship style. A new pastor was called to the church. Within a few months of his arrival, he announced his intention to offer a second Sunday-morning service that would be a blend of the seeker and praise and worship styles. Church members reluctantly agreed to try his proposal, but they did not clearly understand what the changes would entail. In time, tensions began to build between the pastor and the people.

Many of the people felt that their pastor, a relative newcomer, was trying to "steal" their church and change their cherished style of worship. The entire congregation quickly experienced a breakdown of fellowship. Fear, misunderstanding, factions and gossip began to characterize what once had been a community of love. After a year or two of this kind of miserable church life, the pastor abruptly resigned to start a new congregation less than two miles away, taking with him a large group of members who wanted to follow his lead. The remaining members have since picked up the broken pieces. A new pastor who appreciated their original style of worship now leads the church. It has returned to full health.

Given the possible tensions related to worship styles that churches are facing, several questions must be raised. How can a congregation decide the best way for its members to offer corporate praise to God? Is there even such a thing as a right way for a church to worship? Is it ever appropriate for a body of believers to change its worship style? This chapter examines current patterns, future possibilities, intended purposes and practical principles that will help a congregation sort through these questions and find its way through the maze of worship styles.

Patterns
First, I want to take a bird's-eye look at some patterns inherent in

the five styles of worship described in previous chapters. Twelve trends will be highlighted here, each of which will help a church to understand more clearly the worship style it currently practices. These trends can also help a congregation understand what it can expect in the process of considering changing styles or adding another service with a different style. Remember the spectrum from chapter three:

Liturgical	Traditional	Revivalist	Praise & Worship	Seeker

Attitude. As the services move from liturgical to seeker, an attitude of quiet reverence gives way to one of open informality. This change in attitude reflects the change in emphasis from God's transcendence to God's immanence. God's presence moves from "out there" to "right here." "God is great" gives way to "God is good." Holiness is eclipsed by love. Awe is replaced with intimacy.

Mood. Tracking with the change in attitude is a change in mood. With a move from liturgical to praise and worship or seeker service, the mood becomes less solemn and more celebrational, less contemplative and more exuberant, less reflective and more expressive.

Order. Each of these services is planned and structured carefully by ministers, although revivalist services and praise and worship services tend to be more open to "the Spirit's movement." Some old-line Pentecostal services continue to disdain order and to delight in spontaneity. Liturgical and seeker services allow the least amount of flexibility.

Target audience. The liturgical, traditional, and praise and worship styles all seek to lead Christians to worship God. The service is planned primarily with Christians in mind. That is, believers are the target audience. The revivalist and seeker services, however, focus on the non-Christians who may be in attendance. Unbelievers are the target audience. A maxim to remember is this: Worship planning for every style must be done with the target audience in mind.

Congregational singing. Congregational singing undergoes several specific changes as worship styles move from left to right on the worship spectrum. By the time one reaches praise and worship and seeker services, three dramatic changes have occurred. First, hymnals are discarded. The words to songs are now printed in bulletins or projected onto the sanctuary wall. Second, most hymns are replaced by praise choruses and Scripture songs. Third, the traditional minister of music is being augmented or replaced by a praise team. In other words, many churches are choosing to worship without the use of hymnals, hymns or ministers of music!

Special music. Although choirs in most liturgical and some traditional services still sing anthems by older and modern classical composers, revivalist choirs sing gospel and hymn arrangements, and praise teams in praise and worship and seeker services sing contemporary anthems and popular Christian-music arrangements. Clearly, popular music is replacing classical music as worship styles move from left to right.

Musical instruments. While the pipe organ remains the instrument of choice in liturgical worship services, it is augmented or superseded by the electronic organ and the piano in the traditional and revivalist services. Seeker and praise and worship services tend to use an electronic organ, piano, digital synthesizer and jazz ensemble or rock band. Taped musical accompaniment becomes more and more prominent the further one moves away from a liturgical service.

Scripture. Scripture passages are read often in the liturgical service, seldom in the revivalist service and usually no more than once in a service of any of the other three styles.

Offering. The reception of the offering moves from great fanfare in the liturgical service to a "soft sell" approach in the seeker service.

That is, the attitude toward giving changes from expectation to apology.

Sermon. Sermons that follow the lectionary and appeal to the intellect and the social conscience characterize the liturgical service. Bible-centered messages, either expository or topical, generally characterize the traditional and noncharismatic praise and worship services. Evangelistic sermons, either overt or covert, characterize the revivalist and seeker services.

Invitation. The public invitation bears most resemblance to frontier evangelistic services in the revivalist and praise and worship traditions. It is quiet and inconspicuous in the liturgical service. There is no public invitation in most seeker services.

Ordinances. The Lord's Supper receives great emphasis in liturgical worship, whereas baptism gets top billing in the revivalist service. The traditional and praise and worship styles have a balanced emphasis on both ordinances. The seeker service does not include either ordinance.

Possibilities

Given these patterns and trends, how does a church choose from among worship styles? What are the most common options? Is there any conventional wisdom to follow? Are there any pitfalls to avoid?

Single style. In a handful of unique settings, a church can practice one style of worship in a relatively pure form. This can happen only if the ministers and laity deliberately insure that no outside influences dilute their preferred style. I believe that fewer and fewer churches will be able to maintain this kind of stance in the future. Social and cultural plates in our world are shifting so rapidly that sooner or later every church will feel the shock waves. When that happens, the first thing that will be threatened will be its sacrosanct style of worship.

Blended style. Although some churches use only one of these worship models in its pure form, many congregations would identify their worship style as a blend or combination of two or more styles. The most common blends at present are liturgical/traditional, traditional/praise and worship, traditional/revivalist and seeker/praise and worship. These pairs blend most easily because each style shares several commonalities with the other, thereby allowing the creation of a *tertium quid* that becomes acceptable to the worshipers who have grown accustomed to one specific style.

It is not easy, however, for certain styles to blend with others. Churches find it most difficult to blend the seeker style with the traditional or liturgical styles or to blend the praise and worship style with the liturgical. Interestingly, Robert E. Webber claims that there is a "phenomenon of convergence" of charismatic and liturgical worship in some churches.[1] I have not heard about many that have achieved this feat, the exceptions being charismatic Episcopal or Catholic churches. At Christ Charismatic Episcopal Church in Fairfield, Alabama, the Anglican liturgy, centered in the Holy Eucharist, joins forces with charismatic worship expressions to create the blend that Webber describes.

Another example of this kind of worship blend is found at St. Timothy's Catholic Church in Mesa, Arizona. Every Sunday night several hundred teenagers meet together for a "Teen Mass" that lasts two hours. "They sing a free-flowing, energetic liturgy accompanied by a teen worship band. They read Scripture, sing the Lord's Prayer, and gather shoulder to shoulder in a huge huddle around the altar to celebrate the Lord's Supper."[2] This is a true picture of how the ancient liturgy can enhance modern music, and vice versa.

Multiple choices. Unfortunately, some blended services accomplish little more than offending everyone present. As a result, more and more churches are offering multiple services—with different styles at different times—so that members and visitors can worship according to the style that means the most to them. This is becoming more commonplace in my own Baptist tradition. For example, Dunwoody Baptist Church in suburban Atlanta, under the pastoral leadership of Jim Johnson, offers a praise and worship service and a traditional service every Sunday morning. A Saturday-night seeker-sensitive praise and worship service is beginning to draw unchurched baby busters to this innovative congregation. First Baptist Church in Woodbridge, Virginia, located in a suburb of Washington, D.C., is pastored by Ray Bearden. It offers three services on Sunday mornings: a traditional service, a praise and worship service, and a service that blends those two styles. Alan Stanford has led Leesburg Baptist Church in northern Virginia to offer a traditional service, two seeker-sensitive services and a "Gen X" or "Buster" service—all on Sunday morning!

Baptists are not alone on this point, either. I recently read of an Episcopal church in Orange County, California, that offers three distinct worship services every Sunday morning: one is traditional, the second is a blend of praise and worship and seeker-sensitive, and the third is charismatic. We have not seen the end of this "multiple-choice" approach to Sunday services.

I do have one word of warning: some churches that have gone to two separate services with two separate worship styles report the creation of two separate congregations. If this begins to happen, a church can counteract that tendency by intentionally establishing ministries, programs and missions opportunities that bring together members from both services. This will build churchwide fellowship that transcends worship fellowship.

Purposes

As churches are making crucial decisions about how they will worship, they need to keep before them a cardinal truth: More than anything else, the purpose of worship determines the style of worship. In other words, once a congregation decides its reason for gathering together on the Lord's day, the style of worship will follow. Consider how this works with each of the five styles.

First, let's look at liturgical worship. It has a clearly defined purpose: to offer corporate praise to the transcendent God of glory. With this controlling purpose in mind, the minister plans the services so that worshipers can reverently bow before their God in humility and awe. A formal and structured style is fitting. Appropriate attention is given to the fourfold pattern of adoration, confession, proclamation and presentation. The best of classical and traditional music is used. The end determines the means. Purpose informs style.

Next, consider traditional worship. It seeks to achieve the stated twofold purpose of praise and preaching in an atmosphere that is warm but stately. For this to happen, there must be just enough formality to prevent the service from being campy and just enough informality to rescue the service from boredom. Therefore the service order is generally fixed and set. Little room remains for spontaneity once the prelude has begun. But the flexibility of a broader repertoire of music, including gospel hymns and hymn anthems, allows the traditional service to feel more informal than its liturgical counterpart. In other words, style follows purpose.

Now let's look at a praise and worship service. It looks and sounds and feels remarkably different from a traditional or liturgical service. The primary reason is that its purpose is somewhat different. Although all three styles are designed for Christians to worship God, the ways, means and ends differ dramatically. The praise and worship style seeks to bring believers into intimate communion with the immanent Lord of love. This purpose requires the service to be broadly informal, outwardly celebrational and physically expressive. Such a style, punctuated with emotionally charged special music and repetitive chorus singing, frees worshipers to be spontaneous and liberal in their praise.

Again, purpose determines style.

Do you see a common thread running through these three services? To put it simply, if your purpose in joining together for worship is to bless God and to celebrate God's presence, then your worship style will probably be liturgical, traditional or praise and worship. These three styles have one primary thing in common: they are all more God centered than human centered. The differences between them, while not insignificant, are not related to ultimate purpose. They have to do with cultural background, denominational history and musical preference.

What about the revivalist style and the seeker service approach? Both begin with an evangelistic intent, as we have seen, but that is the only similarity. Otherwise the services look, sound and feel completely different from one another. On the one hand, the revivalist style boldly calls sinners to repent. Overt religious images— "the blood of the Lamb," "streets of gold," "the prodigal son"—fill the songs and sermons. Urgent pleadings and protracted invitations give those "under conviction" a little longer to respond to Christ "while there's still time." On the other hand, the seeker style more subtly invites non-Christians or religious seekers to "give Christianity a try." Religious analogies from an earlier day, now considered passé in today's culture, make room for analogies drawn from sports, business, politics and entertainment. Great patience and freedom are extended to those who are giving Christianity serious consideration.

So if your purpose is evangelism, then your service will follow either the revivalist or the seeker style and the orientation will be more human centered than God centered. It is true that the first of these styles will present Christ in overt ways whereas the second will be more covert. It is also true that one style is ready and willing to use persuasion or even pressure to help convert people, while the other follows a soft-sell approach. And it is true that while one will try to instill a fear of hell in you, the other will try to woo you with the benefits of heaven on earth. Yet despite these considerable differences, both styles are aiming at the same goal: to lead unbelievers into a right relationship with God through Christ.

The truth is obvious: No one should underestimate the power of purpose when it comes to worship. As in many other areas of experience, so it is here. The *why* of worship always determines the *what* and the *how.*

Principles
When to stay with a style. Some churches should stay with their current worship style and change nothing. How do you know if your church falls into that category? The best way to answer that question is with another question: Is your church fulfilling its God-given purpose? That is, is your congregation effectively engaged in evangelism, missions, discipleship and ministry? If so, then there may be no good reason to change worship styles. In fact, the evidence suggests that churches that are successfully fulfilling the Great Commission and the Great Commandment also have dynamic, meaningful worship services. One could even go a step further: evangelistic, missionary, disciple-making churches are that way *because* they have dynamic worship services. Who would want to tamper with a service that empowers the people of God to do the work of Christ in the power of the Spirit? Don't change a thing!

Of course, some churches stay with their current worship style for a different reason. They're simply used to it. The church is not on fire for much of anything that is God centered or Christ directed or Spirit empowered. The members simply meet together for fun and food and fellowship. They haven't shared the story of Jesus with a non-Christian in years. They seldom witness a new adult convert getting baptized. They support missions mostly through offerings, not through hands-on efforts. Sunday-school classes may be bulging at the seams, but little in-depth discipleship occurs. It's been a long, long time since God poured out the Spirit in a worship service.

This is comfortable Christianity. If a church wants to remain this way, by all means it should leave its worship style alone. After all, why should anyone rearrange the deck chairs on the *Titanic?*

When to change styles. Occasionally pastors or church leaders evaluate the overall health of the congregation and decide to change worship styles. Let me offer a word of caution here: Changing the style of worship is one of the quickest ways for a pastor to get into hot water with the congregation! Most people don't like change too much anyway, but change in the church frequently rubs people entirely the wrong way. Church members often rejoice in the belief that their church is the only safe refuge in their hectic, mixed-up world. To them, it is the only unchanging institution in a constantly changing culture. The last thing they want is for a pastor to "fool around" with the way they have worshiped for the last several decades!

Therefore any pastor who wants to change worship styles should be forewarned: you're asking for trouble! If you have a weak stomach, leave things alone! Gracious and kind church members can change personalities when someone tinkers with the order of service. They may have loved and praised the pastor just last week, but a few alterations in worship will find them complaining and carping about pastoral authority.

This raises a very important question: What role should the pastor play in determining worship style? How much should the pastor's vision for the church impact congregational worship? Remember that the pastor is called to a church to shepherd the flock of God (1 Pet 5:2). Shepherding demands that the pastor lead the people, feed the people and protect the people. Granted, it is difficult to lead people where they do not want to go, but what the pastor believes is the right direction for the future is still important.

Peter Steinke, Lutheran minister and church consultant, offers significant insight at this point.[3] He admonishes any pastor who leads a congregation in adopting a churchwide vision to prepare for criticism, resistance and even sabotage. When this occurs, the pastor's proper response has five aspects: define yourself (state your vision clearly); regulate your own anxiety (intentionally keep calm); stay connected to others (rather than pull away from them out of anger or hurt); stimulate the congregation's resources (such as creativity and leadership); stay the course (despite others' attempts to get you off track). In other words, the pastor should lead the church from his or her own vision and then patiently wait for the members to follow.[4] Edwin H. Friedman is more blunt: "If a leader will take primary responsibility for his or her own position as 'head' and work to define his or her own goals and self, while *staying in touch* with the rest of the organism, there is a more than reasonable chance that the body will follow."[5]

This is called "leadership by definition." But don't confuse it with hardhearted authoritarianism or arrogant insensitivity. It simply acknowledges two realities: every pastor has a vision for the church, and many pastors will proactively try to lead the congregation accordingly. The pastoral vision encompasses every dimension of church life, including a philosophy of worship and a preference of worship styles. So a pastor often leads a church to change its worship style in order to bring all of congregational life in line with the overall vision for the church. This is leadership by definition.

When to blend styles. If a pastor or church decides neither to stay with nor to change the current worship style, then two possibilities remain. A popular option is to blend two or more styles into a single service. This can happen more easily if the congregation is composed of several generations with several distinct music preferences. Then a blended service can allow each member to worship according to his or her preferred style during a significant portion of the service. The younger generation can sing several praise choruses, while the older generation can still sing many of their favorite hymns. Teenagers can enjoy a dramatic presentation prior to the sermon, while grandparents still get to enjoy a traditional sermon. Youth relish the sound of an offertory played on guitar, while the senior adults still appreciate the organ prelude. In a blended service, all members may worship at least part of the time according to a style that provides the most meaning to them.

But there is a price to pay. That price is tolerating a worship style that you do not like. It may make you feel uncomfortable, as when traditional members hear contemporary music, or it may leave you cold, as when younger members hear classical music. The only way for a blended service not to degenerate into an us-versus-them experience is for sacrificial love to prevail. The biblical answer to this dilemma is found in Philippians 2:4, where the apostle Paul writes, "Each of you should look not only to your own interests, but also to the interests of others." Blended services can work beautifully, but only when each church member wants all other church members to worship in a way that allows them to praise and worship God in a meaningful way.

The challenge of making a blended service meaningful was expressed half a century ago by C. S. Lewis in an essay entitled "On Church Music." He asserted:

There are two musical situations on which I think we can be confident that a blessing rests. One is where a priest or an organist, himself a man of trained and delicate taste, humbly and charitably sacrifices his own (aesthetically right) desires and gives the people humbler and coarser fare than he would wish, in a belief . . . that he can thus bring them to God. The other is where the stupid and unmusical layman humbly and patiently, and above all silently, listens to music which he

cannot, or cannot fully, appreciate, in the belief that it some-
how glorifies God, and that if it does not edify him this must
be his own defect. Neither such a High Brow nor such a Low
Brow can be far out of the way. To both, Church Music will
have been a means of grace; not the music they have liked, but
the music they have disliked. They have both offered, sacri-
ficed, their taste in the fullest sense. But where the opposite
situation arises, where the musician is filled with the pride of
skill or the virus of emulation and looks with contempt on the
unappreciative congregation, or where the unmusical, com-
placently entrenched in their own ignorance and conserva-
tism, look with the restless and resentful hostility of an
inferiority complex on all who would try to improve their taste
—there, we may be sure, all that both offer is unblessed and
the spirit that moves them is not the Holy Ghost.[6]

When to offer new options. If a church cannot handle a blended
service but still wants to allow for a diversity of worship styles, then
it should consider offering new options in worship. A pastor friend
of mine calls this "offering choices, not changes." Many congregations can swallow this pill with just a little explanation. The
explanation (and its criticism) generally goes something like this:
   "After several months [years?] of hearty discussion [bitter fight-
ing?] concerning worship styles [worship wars?], it appears that
the best option [the pastor's choice?] is for our church to offer more
than one worship service on Sunday mornings [why not Sunday
night or Wednesday night?], each having a different style.
   "This decision will allow [force?] each church member to choose
the style that fits him or her best [won't this divide us?]. It will also
allow nonmembers [why are we including them in this decision?],
especially unchurched and unsaved people [why do we have to
grow larger?], to find a service [isn't the new one just entertain-

ment?] that will help them meet God in a dynamic and exciting way [doesn't that sound charismatic or Pentecostal?]."

As you see, not even a multiple-choice approach pleases everyone!

If your church offers a new service with a new style, be sure you cover all the bases first:

☐ When possible, leave the original service at the original time. If that does not work, then schedule it at a convenient time for the probable attenders.

☐ Choose a style for the new service that best matches the portion of your congregation that is calling for changes in worship. Try to match it also to the lifestyle and generational characteristics of unchurched people who live within a two-to-four-mile radius of the church.

☐ Be prepared to locate and enlist worship leaders, especially musicians, to lead the new service. This is doubly important if you are beginning a praise and worship or seeker-style service. The musical demands of these two styles often require liturgical or traditional churches to go outside of their congregation to find the right leadership.

☐ Read books and articles about offering more than one style of worship service. Learn all you can before you start.[7]

☐ Spend several weeks or months planning the first three or four new services. Take the time to do it right. Organize teams around the obvious tasks demanded by the new service. If the added service is either a praise and worship service or a seeker-sensitive service, the planning teams should include drama, music and technology (audio, video and computer).

☐ Once the new service is up and running, keep both groups of worshipers informed about the blessings and benefits of offering multiple styles of worship. This will keep criticism and carping to a minimum and may well breed mutual understanding and appreciation.

Ten

INCLUDING ALL OF THE ELEMENTS

Having Looked at worship and worship styles from several theoretical viewpoints, we now come to a very "earthy" issue—where worship theory steps into the background and worship practice takes center stage. In this chapter we will examine the elements of worship that need to be included in every service, regardless of the style. They are music, prayer, the Word of God, ordinances and sacraments, and the offering. These elements are common to almost every service. They have become the church's nonnegotiables for corporate worship. They should continue to be front and center in worship services today. Let's look at each element in turn.

Music
In his letters, Paul admonished believers to "sing psalms, hymns

and spiritual songs with gratitude in your hearts to God" (Col 3:16). From the psalms in the Old Testament to the Christian hymns in the New Testament (like Phil 2:6-11), the Bible is filled with music that the people of God have sung over the centuries.

The priority of music. Music has always been important to worship. The psalmist wrote,

It is good to praise the LORD
and make music to your name, O Most High. (Ps 92:1)

And the apostle Paul encouraged the earliest Christians to "sing and make music in your heart to the Lord" (Eph 5:19).

These passages make it clear that God holds in high regard the musical dimension of corporate worship. From the experience of Christians throughout the ages, the church has come to value music as one of the most central and powerful elements of worship. Sally Morgenthaler argues that "aside from the Spirit of God, music is the most potent element in a worship service. It has an incredible, matchless capacity to open the human heart to God, accessing the soul more quickly, deeply, and permanently than any other art form or human speech (yes, that includes the message!)."[1] In *Life Together,* Dietrich Bonhoeffer explains, "It is the voice of the Church that is heard in singing together. It is not you that sings, it is the Church that is singing, and you, as a member of the Church, may share in its song."[2] Why does music enhance and enrich worship? Consider these two simple reasons.

First, music touches human emotions in a way that nothing else in life can. God created music to reach us at this deep, otherwise impenetrable level. Were it not for music, our worship would eventually degenerate into a purely rational exercise. But music in worship becomes the bridge from our emotions to God.

Second, music is closely tied to the memory. We often remember more easily what we sing than what we say. Since memory and music are intimately bound together, we discover in worship that we are free to sing to God what we have already learned. We don't have to worry about what to say in the presence of the Most High. We simply repeat what we have already memorized, whether it be "Rock of Ages, Cleft for Me," or "Praise God, from Whom All Blessings Flow" or "Jesus Loves Me, This I Know."

The purposes of music. Music has several purposes in worship, each of which is valid in its own right. First, music is one of the primary means of praising God. Of all the ways by which Christians offer gratitude and adoration to the Lord, music is often considered the most expressive and meaningful. Therefore it is not an appendage but a core value in worship. The great gospel hymn "To God Be the Glory" reaches its climax in the refrain that calls for the people to worship in song:

> Praise the Lord, praise the Lord,
> Let the earth hear his voice.
> Praise the Lord, praise the Lord,
> Let the people rejoice.

We seldom praise God more beautifully in worship than through music.

Second, music is an act of prayer. When sung from the heart, it becomes a vehicle of communication from the human to the divine. Think about some of the best-loved hymns and choruses in this way. "Come, Thou Almighty King" is a petition for God to help us offer the finest praise possible. "Savior, Like a Shepherd Lead Us" asks God to care tenderly for us and to bring us safely to our destination. "God of Grace and God of Glory" earnestly begs God to grant wisdom and courage to us as disciples of Jesus while we live in this world. "I Love You, Lord" directly offers a prayer of adoration to God. Understood rightly, music in worship is lyrical prayer.

Third, music is an important means of teaching biblical truth to the people of God. As mentioned above, it may be a truism to say that we remember what we sing, but our remembering seems to be an empirical fact of experience. I learned to sing "Jesus Loves the Little Children" as a little boy. When the American civil rights turmoil boiled over in the 1960s, I knew where I stood. My belief in the fundamental equality of all races came not from any specific biblical insight that I learned in Sunday school but from the confidence that children of every color "are precious in his sight." A child's song had educated me about ethics. Similarly, when I went to seminary, I began wrestling with the doctrine of the Trinity in a class on systematic theology. When I had struggled with the mystery of the Godhead for as long as my finite mind could endure, I could eventually relax and rest in those words I had learned to sing in church as a young boy: "Holy, holy, holy! Lord God Almighty! . . . God in three persons, blessed Trinity!" A great hymn had taught me theology.

While hymnody has indeed been one of the primary teachers of the church, the words we sing do not always match the theology we profess. Fisher Humphreys, professor of theology at Beeson Divinity School, once pointed out to me the discrepancy in two popular Christmas carols. The second stanza of "Away in a Manger" states that "little Lord Jesus, no crying he makes." Since Jesus "had to be made like his brothers in every way" (Heb 2:17) and since all babies cry from time to time, it is reasonable to conclude that Jesus did in fact cry as an infant. Yet we sing this carol every Christmas, oblivious to the words that we do not really believe. Also, stanza three of "Angels We Have Heard on High" asks Jesus' parents to help us as we sing: "Mary, Joseph, lend your aid, while in love our hearts we raise." Praying to the Blessed Virgin Mary is foreign to every Free Church congregation around, yet we continue to sing this popular hymn, even when its theology does not match ours.

Fourth, music serves as a confession of faith. Consider the three defining moments of the life of Jesus Christ: his birth, death and resurrection. One of the favorite hymns of the Advent season is "Joy to the World." What Isaac Watts has given to the church through this hymn is a confident confession of our belief that the baby Jesus is really the long-expected Lord and Savior of the world. We boldly sing,

> Joy to the world! the Lord is come . . .
> Joy to the earth! the Savior reigns . . .
> He rules the world with truth and grace.

Watts also captured in lyrics the church's understanding of Christ's death in "When I Survey the Wondrous Cross." Consider these words as a confession of faith:

> See, from his head, his hands, his feet,
> Sorrow and love flow mingled down;
> Did e'er such love and sorrow meet,
> Or thorns compose so rich a crown?

Likewise, Charles Wesley confessed the church's Easter faith when he wrote:

> Christ the Lord is ris'n today, Alleluia! . . .
> Lives again our glorious King, Alleluia! . . .
> Love's redeeming work is done, Alleluia!

Now I understand why one of my seminary professors once said, "I believe only what I can sing!"

Finally, music provides worshipers with a genuine means of active participation in worship. One hymnologist has written, "Hymns are for us Dissenters what the liturgy is for the Anglican."[3] If that is true, then all congregations from the Free Church tradition need music in order to keep worship from hardening into a lifeless observance.

The types of music. The Pauline letters reveal at least three types of music prevalent in the early church: "psalms, hymns and spiritual songs" (Eph 5:19; Col 3:16). "Psalms" likely refer to portions of the Hebrew Psalter set to music for worship. They may have been more objective, God-centered expressions of musical worship. Modern examples include "All People That on Earth Do Dwell," the classic hymn based on Psalm 100, and "Bless His Holy Name," the popular chorus by Andrae Crouch based on Psalm 103.

In the first-century church, the word *hymn* may have been used in the same sense that we use it today: human words of praise to God for his grace and goodness. These compositions can reflect numerous Christian themes, including creation, redemption, resurrection, the church and so on. Some of the church's great hymns include "All Hail the Power of Jesus' Name," "Joyful, Joyful, We Adore Thee," "For the Beauty of the Earth" and "O Sacred Head, Now Wounded."

Today's equivalents of "spiritual songs" probably include gospel hymns, Negro spirituals from the black church and many of the praise choruses that are so prominent today. Inspiring and emotionally charged, these songs tend to be primarily human centered, experience oriented and subjective. They are testimonials and devotionals put to music that reflect on some aspect of the Christian life. Popular "spiritual songs" today include "Just As I Am," "Standing in the Need of Prayer," "God Is So Good" and "You Are My All in All."

Considerations when choosing music. Music should be an expression of worship in every aspect of the service. That is, music can communicate adoration, thanksgiving, confession, testimony, prayer, proclamation and dedication. For the richest possible worship, we must use music in as many ways as possible, including instrumental music, congregational music and music for choirs, ensembles and solos.

In choosing music for worship, the worship planner should consider several goals. First, choose music with a specific intention and purpose in mind. Songs selected at random or without valid reason do nothing to enrich worship.

Second, choose music that brings people into closer contact with God, with self and with the world. One of the purposes and values of worship is that it focuses our thoughts and lives on the God above us, the Christ beside us and the Spirit within us. Music tends to sharpen this focus.

Third, choose music that balances objectivity and subjectivity. A diet of purely objective music, directed solely at God, may rob the worshiper of the personal, emotional impact that worship is intended to bring. At the same time, a diet of merely subjective music may succeed in idolizing religious experience to the point of ignoring the nature and authority of God. The clear solution is to plan a well-balanced diet of both objective and subjective music, regardless of the style.

Fourth, choose music that balances the familiar with the less familiar. To use only familiar music restricts the musical "canon" of a congregation. It also runs the risk of replacing meaning with sentimentalism. But to err in the direction of using only unfamiliar music runs the risk of having novelty for novelty's sake.

Finally, choose music that is doctrinally sound and experientially valid. An easy and effective way to evaluate those criteria is to ask the questions, Are the words to this song true? and Are they deep enough to be a meaningful guide for Christians in their devotional lives? If the answer to both questions is yes, then the song has passed the test.

Warnings about choosing music. For all of its value in worship, music also is the point at which the five styles differ most. More importantly, music is the aspect of worship that leads to conflict more than any of the other elements. Rick Warren writes from experience when he says,

> Once you have decided on the style of music you're going to
> use in worship, you have set the direction of your church in
> far more ways than you realize. It will determine the kind of
> people you attract, the kind of people you keep, and the kind
> of people you lose.[4]

Music has great power to unite or divide a congregation. Be careful
how you use this kind of power.

Prayer

The initial converts to Christianity "devoted themselves to . . .
prayer" (Acts 2:42). Whenever followers of Jesus gathered together
in his name, they regularly "raised their voices together in prayer
to God" (Acts 4:24).

Presuppositions about prayer. What is the relation of prayer to
worship? John Killinger gets right to the point when he asserts,
"Christian worship is prayer. That's what our whole service is
about."[5] His point is well made. In truth, not one aspect of worship
is excluded from this claim. All of worship is prayer: the hymns, the
offering, the sermon and all the rest—not to mention the prayers
themselves!

But when a prayer is offered in a congregational setting, is that
prayer a private or a public act of worship? I think it is both. Prayer in
worship combines in a delightful way both individual and corporate
communion with God. The "pray-er" must personalize each prayer,
or true worship has not occurred for that person as a child of God. But
the pray-er also must remember that he or she is "surrounded by such
a great cloud of witnesses" (Heb 12:1) in the service who are also
praying simultaneously. This reminds worshipers that the unique
identity of the church as the body of Christ, made up of many members,
may be seen and experienced in worship.

Principles of prayer. Christians who lead in prayer during worship services should consider the following principles as faithful guidelines for helping them fulfill this high calling in a way that honors the Lord and helps the worshipers. First, pray to God. This probably sounds too elementary even to mention. But public pray-ers can and do fall into numerous traps here on a regular basis. The most frequent is to pray about church programs rather than pray to God: for example, "As we depart today, may everyone gathered here remember to attend the special revival services beginning tomorrow night!" Another misstep occurs when we pray *about* God, as in "We're here to thank the Lord for this beautiful day!" We should address all prayers to God alone.

Second, prayers should be offered reverently and respectfully. After all, we are calling on the name of the Holy One of Israel, who is also the God and Father of our Lord Jesus Christ. The exact opposite of what I am suggesting occurred one evening several years ago when I had just finished speaking to a group of ministerial students about the meaning and priority of worship. At the end of the meeting I asked one of the students to close in prayer. His words came out like this: "Lord, we just wanna say, Wow! Thanks for hanging out with us tonight! Amen." This student obviously forgot to whom he was praying! How do we correct this error? The solution does not require reverting to seventeenth-century English, nor does it call for Christians to speak unnaturally when addressing God. What is needed is nothing less than a spirit of gentle humility, which will issue forth in appropriate reverence and dignity.

Third, be simple and straightforward when you lead in prayer. The two equal but opposite errors to avoid here are what Ralph P. Martin calls "nursery" praying—that is, a childish kind of praying that embarrasses the other worshipers—and "a convoluted or esoteric style of praying that leaves the people confused and threatened."[6] The goal to aim at is clear, direct, sincere prayer.

Fourth, as often as possible use corporate language when you are leading others in prayer. Lean heavily on first-person plural pronouns like *we, us* and *our*. For example, worshipers can easily identify and follow along with a pray-er who says, "We ask you to prepare our hearts for worship, O Lord. Please refresh our spirits with your Spirit. For our prayer is in Jesus' name. Amen." But it is far more difficult to feel included if the pray-er stays in the first person singular and prays, "I just ask you, Lord, to prepare my heart for worship. Please refresh my spirit with your Spirit. And I pray this in Jesus' name. Amen." After all, those who *lead* in prayer must both represent and guide those whom they seek to bring into the presence of God in prayer. And representation and guidance require identification and inclusion. Bonhoeffer explains that "the free prayer in the common devotion should be the prayer of the fellowship and not that of the individual who is praying. It is his responsibility to pray for the fellowship. . . . He prays as a brother among brothers."[7]

Fifth, make sure that every prayer has a specific purpose. All prayers do not and should not sound the same or follow the same pattern or have similar wording. Invocations at the beginning of a service are designed to ask the Lord to meet us in a personal way, so that we might truly fulfill our purpose of gathering together to worship God. Prayers of confession gather up the unconfessed sins of the whole body of believers and present them to God, asking him to remove them as hindrances to effective fellowship and worship. Offertory prayers dedicate the monetary gifts we give to the glory of God. Pastoral prayers generally include elements of praise, thanksgiving, petition and commitment. The benediction closes the service by assuring the congregation of God's continued blessing upon them as they depart. Realizing that every prayer in a worship service is different from the others helps keep ministers and lay leaders focused on the reason they are praying.

Sixth, use biblical patterns and biblical language to structure and strengthen prayer. By following the order of the Lord's Prayer, for instance, the worship leader will praise our Heavenly Father before mentioning our need for daily bread and will submit to God's will before asking to be saved from evil. In addition, using meaningful biblical phrases will not only enrich public prayer but also save the pray-er from using so many tired and worn-out religious clichés, like "bless the gift and the giver" and "be with all of those who could not be here today." The Bible should be our authority "in all matters of faith and practice," including our public prayers. Again Bonhoeffer is a faithful guide: "Relating the prayer to one of the Scripture readings will also prove helpful for liberating the free prayer from the caprice of subjectivity."[8]

Seventh, use your natural voice, vocabulary and cadence. Ministers are often tempted to try to impress the congregation with theological prowess and "the voice of God." Instead, the one who leads in public prayer should simply relax and be himself or herself. Bonhoeffer reminds us that in the midst of fellow Christians, "all fear of one another, all timidity about praying freely in one's own words in the presence of others may be put aside where in all simplicity and soberness the common, brotherly prayer is lifted to God by one of the brethren."[9] The apostle Paul understood this principle very well. To the Corinthian Christians he wrote, "But we have this treasure in jars of clay to show that this all-surpassing power is from God and not from us" (2 Cor 4:7). In prayer, true power and beauty reside not in the one who prays but in the One to whom we pray.

Finally, public prayer deserves preparation. Two implications follow. First, I believe that it is wise to spend time thinking about what you want to say in your prayer *before* you say it. Anticipate the intent of the prayer and some of the phrases you might use. Write down at least a skeleton outline of what you want to say so that your prayer can be most meaningful to those who are trying to follow you into "the Most Holy Place." Preparation for public prayer does not ruin prayer. On the contrary, "prayer, even though it be free, will be determined by a certain internal order. It is not the chaotic outburst of a human heart but the prayer of an inwardly ordered fellowship."[10] Second, not many people like to be surprised in a worship service by being called on to pray without advance notice. Common courtesy suggests that ministers inform church members ahead of time about a request to lead in public prayer.

The Word of God

In one of his last letters, Paul gave Timothy the following charge: "Until I come, devote yourself to the public reading of scripture, to preaching and to teaching" (1 Tim 4:13). No worship service is complete unless the Word of God has been read and proclaimed.

Reading the Word. The public reading of Scripture, without human comment, deserves practice and respect in worship. Because worship is intended to be a dialogue between God and God's children, the reading of the Bible has great value. This may be the only time that God's Word is allowed to speak for itself in a worship service vis-à-vis the interpretation of the Word offered in hymns and sermons.

Scripture readings can be used effectively at numerous points during a service: as a call to worship, during times of confession and intercession, before the sermon and as a benediction. But whenever Scriptures are read, the passages should reflect the beauty and variety of the whole Bible, from Genesis to Revelation.

Some churches prefer to use a solo reader for Scripture, usually a minister. Other churches have discovered the value of lay readers and congregational reading. Regardless of the approach adopted, the goal is for the people of God to hear the Word of God in all of its grandeur and glory.

Now we come to a tricky question: what is an appropriate length for the Scripture reading? I believe there are two extremes to be avoided: a single verse (although that is appropriate for the offertory sentence, which I will mention later) and a long chapter. It is best to read a single unit of Scripture, which usually equates to a gospel story or parable, an epistolary paragraph, a prophetic oracle or a shorter psalm. In general, ten to fifteen verses is a good length for public reading, but that is merely a rule of thumb, not a law written in stone. Bonhoeffer holds the conviction "that brief verses cannot and should not take the place of reading the Scripture as a whole. . . . Holy Scripture does not consist of individual passages; it is a unit and is intended to be used as such."[11]

Finally, we should consider which translation of the Bible should be read. Unless a congregation has an unwritten but highly revered tradition that demands all Scripture readings come from a particular translation, feel free to select from among several versions. The most common are the King James Version and the New King James Version, the Revised Standard Version and the New Revised Standard Version, the New English Bible and the New Revised English Bible, the New International Version and the New American Standard Bible. Do not overlook the simple power of the Contemporary English Version, the flair of J. B. Phillips's paraphrase and the down-to-earth idioms of Eugene Peterson's *The Message*.

Preaching the Word. If music is the soul of Christian worship and prayer is its spirit, then preaching is often considered its heart. Certainly this is true for most evangelical churches and Free churches within the Protestant tradition. But however much we exalt the role of preaching, we err if we regard the sermon as the sum-total of the service. Preaching is *not* the distilled essence of Christian worship. Without a doubt, it is the primary means by which God's Word is proclaimed to God's people, but it is only a part of the dialogue of worship. Preaching that is divorced from worship is monologue, and monologue is never worship!

Although no biblical mandate exists concerning what a pastor should preach during the course of a year (or a lifetime), the following principles have aided me in developing a plan for preaching. First, preach from both the Old Testament and the New Testament. The same God reveals himself and his purposes in each testament, so the Christian preacher can confidently draw from the entire Bible for sermon texts. And when the pastor gets lost in some of the difficult and thorny passages in the Old Testament, an informed Christ-centered hermeneutic will be a faithful guide. As Eugene Peterson points out, "All the words of Scripture are contextually coherent in the word made flesh, Jesus."[12]

Second, to stay honest with the Bible as the "whole counsel of God," follow a specific preaching plan that will end up covering as much of the Bible as possible over several years. Many pastors turn to the Common Lectionary or the Revised Common Lectionary,[13] which is a three-year cycle of Scripture passages that suggests two Old Testament texts and two New Testament texts per Sunday. Using this as a guide, the conscientious pastor can plan a year's worth of preaching in such a way that church members are exposed to the rich variety of Holy Scripture in its entirety. The Lectionary also lends itself to sermon series based on Bible books.

Third, a congregation needs to hear preaching that comes from the central passages of Christianity, those that have guided and informed the church for almost two millennia. A sample list of these golden texts from the Old Testament alone would include the story of creation and fall; the call and life of Abraham; the story cycles of Isaac, Jacob and Joseph; the Exodus from Egypt; the Ten Commandments; the wilderness wanderings; the entry into the Promised Land; the story cycles of Samuel, Saul and David; the lives of Elijah and Elisha; the classic prophecies of Isaiah, Amos, Hosea and Jeremiah; the fall of Israel and of Judah; the faith of Daniel; the return from exile; the most meaningful psalms; and wisdom from Job and from Proverbs. What about the New Testament? It offers the life of Jesus in narrative form, from birth to ascension; the primary teachings of Jesus; the meaning of his birth, death and resurrection; the coming of the Spirit at Pentecost; the trials and triumphs of the earliest Christian leaders, especially Peter, Stephen and Paul; the "red letter" passages out of Paul's epistles; the most significant sections from the general epistles; and highlights from Revelation. No preacher who takes a serious look at the breadth and depth of the Bible's message will ever lack material for preaching!

Fourth, churches need to hear sermons on both doctrine and duty, theology and ethics, belief and behavior. Preaching should guide God's people along "the paths of righteousness," and this necessarily includes the mandates to both "change how you *think*" and "change how you *live*." Theology without ethics degenerates into religious rationalism; ethics without theology produces mindless moralism and loveless legalism. It is the preacher's responsibility to challenge both the mind and the heart of the people who come to worship services.

Finally, preach to the needs of the congregation. Sermons that address genuine needs and critical concerns carry on in the great tradition of the Old Testament prophets and the New Testament parables.

Ordinances and Sacraments
Neither the word *ordinance* nor the word *sacrament* is found in the New Testament. Yet for almost twenty centuries they have been the most common words used to describe the meaning of the two great enacted parables of the church: baptism and the Lord's Supper. Although not biblical words in the strictest sense, they refer to important actions that find their value by pointing to a reality beyond themselves. To understand this more fully, consider the following definitions.

According to the Book of Common Prayer, a sacrament may be defined as "an outward and visible sign of an inward and spiritual grace given unto us . . . by Christ himself."[14] A fuller definition comes from the Westminster Confession of Faith: "A sacrament is a holy ordinance instituted by Christ, wherein, by sensible signs, Christ, and the benefits of the new covenant, are represented, sealed, and applied to believers."[15] John Calvin defined a sacrament as "an outward sign by which the Lord seals on our consciences the promises of his good will toward us in order to sustain the weakness of our faith; and we in turn attest our piety toward him."[16] Franklin M. Segler offers a common Baptist understanding when he defines ordinances as "symbols of God's revelation, . . . not vehicles of God's grace."[17]

To summarize, an ordinance or a sacrament is an element of worship in which a basic physical substance and a simple human action represent and communicate the grace and the Word of God. Certain necessary components must exist for an act to qualify as a sacrament or an ordinance. Robert G. Rayburn claims that there are three explicit prerequisites: "the scriptural words of the institution," "the material elements used to establish the sign" and "the physical action required."[18] We can add two other implicit requirements: persons participating by a response of faith and a worshiping community. Where these factors intersect, corporate worship is enriched as the message of the gospel is reenacted in clear and unmistakable ways and as followers of Jesus are reminded of the benefits that are theirs through his life, death and resurrection.

Baptism. The New Testament refers often to baptism. According to Ralph P. Martin, these references can be organized into several emphases.[19] First, baptism was hallowed by both John the Baptist and Jesus of Nazareth (Mt 3:1-7, 13-17; 28:19). Second, every follower of Jesus apparently received baptism either by John or in Jesus' name (Acts 19:1-5). Third, because baptism was "in the name of Jesus," it became what Martin calls "the badge of discipleship" for early Christians (Acts 2:38; 1 Cor 1:12-16). Fourth, baptism was the means of entry, or rite of initiation, into the early church (Acts 2:41). Fifth, baptism was a focal point of unity among the first Christians (Eph 4:5). Sixth, baptism pointed to the reality of the new creation, with the primary images being those of burial and resurrection and of new garments (Rom 6:1-4; Gal 3:27). Finally, baptism generally occurred in conjunction with faith, trust or repentance, suggesting that baptism was generally reserved for believers (Acts 2:38, 41; 18:8). (Because I am a Baptist, I espouse believers' baptism by immersion rather than infant baptism by sprinkling. But I refuse to make this a test of either orthodoxy or fellowship. The common Christian confession for almost two thousand years has been "Jesus is Lord." That alone is the essential and ultimate basis of unity for Christians.)

Given the priority of baptism in the New Testament, how can a church make it a priority in worship? To begin with, baptism must occupy a central place in the drama of worship and must not be relegated to prologue or epilogue. I know of two churches in which new members are baptized during the organ prelude, while people are entering the sanctuary to find a seat! I prefer to place baptism in the heart of the service and to couple it with a hymn or a Scripture reading or even the sermon. One pastor I know devoted the entire morning service to baptism, with Scripture readings, prayers, testimonies and songs magnifying the importance of this event. Another way to elevate baptism to its rightful place of honor is to celebrate it in the same service with the Lord's Supper.

Additionally, the church should teach baptismal candidates clearly about the meaning of both salvation and baptism.[20] This return to the practice of early catechesis will enrich the sacred experience of baptism for all who participate.

When candidates enter the water, I think it is appropriate for the minister to introduce them to the congregation, giving not only their name but also pertinent background information on their decision to follow Jesus Christ and join the church. Following the introduction, the minister should ask the candidate to publicly profess "Jesus is Lord," which has been the standard confession of faith for Christians since the first century. The minister may also ask the candidate, if he or she has been previously informed, to give a brief testimony about being born again and desiring to be baptized in Jesus' name.

Many people find worship to be more meaningful when they participate actively. In a service of baptism, the congregation can participate in several ways. They can sing a chorus or a refrain from a hymn as the candidate comes out of the water, or they can say amen at that point.

Finally, where the occasion permits, consider celebrating afterward with a church fellowship in honor of those who have just been baptized. In a church where I once served as pastor, we baptized on Sunday evenings and followed this pattern. My father-in-law, Bill O'Brien, used to baptize on Sunday mornings and then celebrate an all-church "love feast" after the service, at which time the Lord's Supper was served for the first time to those who were just baptized. A little creativity and planning can go a long way toward making baptism a significant part of Christian worship.

The Lord's Supper. Like baptism, the Lord's Supper is prominent in the New Testament, occupying front and center stage in the three Synoptic Gospels and receiving extended treatment on two occasions in 1 Corinthians. The basic New Testament emphases on the Lord's Supper include the following items.[21] First, the Lord's Supper was hallowed by both Jesus and the Twelve (Mt 26:17-30 and parallels). Second, it was regarded as a memorial to Jesus, but never a funeral (1 Cor 11:23-25). Third, in itself it was the gospel proclamation (1 Cor 11:26). Fourth, it was an eschatological pledge, reminding believers of Jesus' certain return (Mt 26:29; 1 Cor 11:26). Fifth, it was to be a time of self-examination (1 Cor 11:27-32). Sixth, the Lord's Supper was a thanksgiving—the Greek word *eucharistos* means "grateful" or "thankful"—to Christ (1 Cor 10:16; 11:24). Seventh, it was a communion with Christ (1 Cor 10:16). Eighth, it was also a focal point of Christian unity (1 Cor 10:17). Finally, the Lord's Supper was mysterious but not magical. That is, the words of institution ("This—my body, this—my blood") point to a profound mystery but do not suggest any kind of wizardry or sorcery.

The challenge for worship leaders, especially ministers, is to design and lead worship services that highlight the Lord's Supper in such a way that this extraordinary ordinance can have the greatest impact possible on worshipers. As with baptism, the first place to start is by making the Lord's Supper central to the service. This can be done by placing it within the heart of the worship drama rather than by treating it like an afterthought or an appendix.

It is always helpful to give worshipers an opportunity to prepare their hearts to partake of the elements. This preparation can take several forms, including confession, prayer, Scripture readings, congregational singing or special music. One night several years ago, I was unexpectedly and profoundly moved at a Christmas Eve candlelight Communion service. The minister began repeating Scripture verses while the bread and cup were being distributed. From memory he quoted verse after verse. Many of the passages confronted me with God's grace and demands. Before I knew it I found myself quietly crying as I confessed my sin and received God's grace. That pastor's advance planning and preparation allowed me to meet the risen Christ that night in a powerful way.

Many congregations from the Free Church tradition need to rethink the frequency with which they offer the Lord's Supper. Some churches do it quarterly, others do it bimonthly, a handful do it monthly. My opinion is that we need to spread the table of the Lord more often than every two or three months. I contend that monthly celebration of the Lord's Supper yields rich and lasting benefits for church members. We need tangible reminders of God's gift in Christ at least that often! The scheduling should include the celebration of this ordinance on the highest and holiest days of the church year, including Christmas Eve, Maundy Thursday, Palm Sunday and Easter Sunday, as well as Thanksgiving and a church's anniversary Sunday.

Although it may sound unusual, I am an advocate of using fresh bread and drink whenever possible. Stale crackers, taken from an undated box that was shipped from denominational headquarters, communicate something other than vitality. Let fresh bread suggest the Bread of Life! Let fresh drink point to the One who said, "If anyone is thirsty, let him come to me" (Jn 7:37). The drama of the moment can become even more real if the minister uses the active symbols of literally breaking a loaf of bread and pouring out the drink.

In order to keep the Lord's Supper as meaningful as possible, churches have employed great creativity. To highlight the self-reflective dimension of the Supper, some churches partake of the bread and the cup in total silence. Other churches couple it with a church dinner in order to emphasize the dimension of fellowship. One church may pass the elements to the members, who are seated, as a way of remembering how Christ served the disciples at the Last Supper. Another church may invite the members to come to the table in order to signify that discipleship always means coming to Christ. Dignified creativity prevents us from falling into the trap where familiarity breeds contempt.

Offering

Although often overlooked as a legitimate act of worship, the collection of the offering provides an opportunity for every worshiper to participate actively. It should be seen as an act of worship in which the believer gives money or another material gift to the kingdom of God as a sign of giving the whole of life to God.

The spiritual values of collecting an offering are many. First, giving to God's work helps Christians learn to integrate the material and the spiritual. Second, it lets the believer put his or her faith to work in a very practical way. Third, the proceeds of the offering provide a concrete means of ministry to others. Fourth, as the story of the poor widow indicates, an offering provides us with a tangible way to express our love to God (Mk 12:41-44). Fifth, faithful giving helps us to tame our greed and selfishness. Sixth, giving an offering serves as a reminder of God's ultimate ownership of our entire lives. Finally, the act of giving symbolizes the offering of our total selves to God.

In order to make the offering as meaningful as possible, some churches are moving the collection from the middle of the service to the end, after the sermon and the hymn of invitation. They believe that the offering thus becomes a response to the Word of God and to the entire service of worship. Whenever the offering is collected, however, I want to commend a particular practice that can enhance worship. Let whoever says the offertory prayer read a pertinent passage of Scripture related to stewardship immediately prior to the prayer. This simple practice keeps the purpose of the offering and the call to generosity before the congregation on a weekly basis.

Eleven

PREPARING FOR WORSHIP

A MEANINGFUL WORSHIP SERVICE SELDOM HAPPENS BY OSMOSIS. It requires careful preparation. This involves the three steps of planning, leading and evaluating the service.[1]

Planning the Service

Define your purpose. The first step in planning worship is to ask the simple but profound question "What are we doing here?"

This question points to a central but often unnoticed truth about worship, namely that purpose is all-determinative. A congregation's purpose in worship may be clearly articulated or poorly formulated; it may be anchored in a specific historical tradition or self-consciously ahistorical; it may take its cues from clear biblical teachings or reveal a deep biblical illiteracy; it may be captive to culture or countercultural. But in all of these cases, the final shape and form of worship will be determined more by its purpose than by any other factor.

Most of the time a church's purpose for worshiping depends on certain presuppositions that govern all decisions related to the service. These presuppositions are in reality foundational beliefs and core convictions that reflect ultimate values held by the church. They may be intentional, but more often than not they are subconscious and unexamined ideas that come from a congregation's essential identity.

After years of careful reflection, I have reached a tentative conclusion about the goal of worship. This is a working summary of how I currently view the primary and secondary purposes of worship.

☐ The primary purpose of worship is to offer praise and thanksgiving to God for who he is and for what he has done (adoration) and to reaffirm our love for and commitment to him (dedication).

☐ The secondary purposes of worship are to find and follow Jesus' way of life (pastoral care), to submit to God's standards and perspective on life (ethics), to build up and unite the body of Christ (fellowship) and to proclaim God's love and mercy to unbelievers (evangelism).

This purpose statement reveals my differences with the revivalist and seeker styles described above. I understand the purpose of worship to be primarily God centered. Not all Christians, not even all of the people in congregations where I have pastored, would agree with my assessment of the goals of worship. But the fact that we would differ only underlines my thesis: everyone possesses certain notions, usually very strong, about why we worship and how that worship should look, sound and feel. For most believers, worship has one or two ultimate concerns. Any other effects of worship must be considered penultimate.

The goal in a local congregation, of course, is for the members to recognize their own preconceived ideas about worship and to evaluate them in light of basic biblical teachings about worship so that they can adjust their ideas as they grow in knowledge.

So I offer a new beatitude: Blessed is the church that knows, *really knows,* why it gathers together on the Lord's Day for corporate worship!

Establish priorities. Once the purpose of worship is determined, someone must take the initiative to plan weekly services that will reflect these overall goals. Usually this is the responsibility of the pastor or the minister of music. Whoever has this assignment must make it a priority, because high-quality Christian worship seldom happens accidentally or without planning. At least one person should see worship planning as a major part of his or her weekly schedule.

I make it a practice to give to the minister of music a list of my sermon topics and texts every three or four months. With that information before him, he selects music—congregational, choral and solo—to complement the sermon and to match the theme of each service. Then he and I meet for at least an hour every Tuesday or Wednesday to plan the upcoming Sunday-morning service in detail. Our primary goal is to design the service so that it will lead the entire congregation into the very presence of God when they gather on the Lord's Day.

When Sunday morning arrives, all of us who have a leadership role in the service gather ahead of time to review our parts. We talk through the service, from prelude to postlude. And every Sunday, without fail, we discover that we would have made some obvious gaffes during the actual service had we not taken that time of final review. The value of this final review, where all worship leaders "get on the same page," is hard to overestimate.

Follow the principles. Several principles guide those who take worship planning seriously and realize its profound importance.

These principles take the form of knowing the overall pattern, knowing the theme, knowing the time and knowing the people.

The first principle is knowing the pattern of the service. Regardless of the style of worship your church embraces, a common pattern found both in the Bible and in church history can serve as a model in planning. This biblical and historic pattern consists of four emphases.

We begin with *praise* and adoration of God. Since God is the one who has called us to worship, our first duty is to "praise his holy name" (Ps 103:1). This can be accomplished through prayer; through choral, solo or instrumental music; and through the reading of Scripture, especially the psalms.

Following praise and adoration is *prayer* in its many forms. The early church was encouraged at this very point: "I urge, then, first of all, that requests, prayers, intercession and thanksgiving be made for everyone" (1 Tim 2:1). Today this can happen through the invocation, prayer of confession, pastoral prayer and offertory prayer.

Next is the *proclamation* of the Word of God. This takes place when Holy Scripture is read and when special music is sung, but above all it happens when the sermon is preached. Preaching has been of utmost importance to worship ever since Timothy was instructed to "preach the Word . . . in season and out of season" (2 Tim 4:2). No significant Christian tradition or community, other than the Quakers, holds that corporate worship can occur without the proclamation of the Word of God.

After God has spoken through his Word, the last act of worship can take place: the *presentation* of life. For those Christians influenced by frontier revivalism, this is often translated into a public invitation or an altar call, at which time people are invited to make public decisions about conversion, discipleship or church membership. Also included here are the hymn of commitment and the benediction.

This fourfold pattern of worship—praise, prayer, proclamation and presentation—has both guided and protected Christian worship for centuries. It continues to provide a basic planning model for worship leaders today. It is flexible enough to be adapted to any style, but it is faithful enough to the biblical and historical emphases of worship that it will ensure the integrity of any service for which it is the model.

Knowing the theme is the second principle. Every service of worship should have one or two overarching themes that provide continuity for each element included that day. For example, suppose you wanted to plan a service that would lead the congregation to trust the Lord in the midst of trials. In order to keep focused on that aim throughout the service, you could weave together hymns, prayers, Scriptures, special music and a sermon that all revolve around that theme. This could result in choosing hymns like "Great Is Thy Faithfulness" and "It Is Well with My Soul" and a chorus like "In His Time"; selecting Scriptures such as Psalm 63 and James 1:2-5; and choosing as the sermon text the Gospel story of Jesus' quieting the storm. Approaching worship planning this way helps to insure that the experience of Sunday worship will be integrated and purposeful, not helter-skelter.

Principle three is knowing the time. Knowing the time—where you are in the Christian year—can help to determine how we worship. In fact, a Christian view of time affects one's philosophy, practice and planning of worship.

Numerous churches, especially those within the revivalist tradition, have never thought about the relation of worship to time. But as Robert E. Webber has cautioned, "If the Christian world is to break from secularism, it must examine the unthinking way it has adopted a secular way of reckoning time in worship."[2] His concern is that many churches, although probably without forethought, have chosen to make national holidays and civic celebrations the basis of their worship year. These worship services are planned around worldly themes such as New Year's Day, Valentine's Day, Memorial Day, Mother's Day, Father's Day, Independence Day, Labor Day and Thanksgiving. These days are certainly fun to celebrate with family and friends, but should they form the backbone of the worship year? Should they determine the focus and content of a congregation's most significant action? If not, is there another way to let a Christian view of time inform and guide worship?

A practice common to the Roman Catholic Church, most mainline Protestant churches and a growing number of evangelical churches is following the Christian year. This means that the major events of the life of Christ and of the early church become the central framework for planning corporate worship. This "Christian calendar" may be found in the Common Lectionary or the Revised Common Lectionary. Lectionaries help in planning worship services around biblical passages that highlight our Lord's life, specifically his birth, ministry, passion, resurrection and the sending of the Spirit. Therefore the lectionary organizes the fifty-two Sundays of the year around the themes of

☐ Advent (the four weeks prior to Christmas)

☐ Epiphany (four to eight Sundays from January 6 to Ash Wednesday)

☐ Lent (forty weekdays and six Sundays from Ash Wednesday through Good Friday)

☐ Easter (seven weeks beginning with Easter),

☐ Pentecost (from fifty days after Easter to the beginning of Advent)

Each Sunday has assigned to it three or four biblical texts: one or two from the Old Testament, one from the gospels and one from the epistles. All of the passages are related to the seasonal theme for that Sunday. Taken week by week, these passages provide a common topic around which sermon, prayers, hymns and other music can revolve. When considered annually, the lectionary provides a coherent whole for the church's worship. A three-year cycle of texts broadens the biblical canon for both preacher and congregation.

Whether or not one should slavishly follow the lectionary is not the issue here. What matters is that Jesus Christ really is the center of time and the One who gives meaning to time. If this is true, then his life should guide our worship more directly. Adopting or adapting the Christian year for worship is one significant way in which congregations can do that corporately.

One last principle can help in planning worship: know the people. The more you know your congregation, the more effective your worship planning will be. For example, what is your church's history? What are the primary needs of the people? What is their dominant culture? What congregational stories best describe their basic values? Why do they come to worship in the first place, and what are they really looking for? Finding answers to these kinds of questions will help you to customize worship for the people in whose service you have been placed.

Leading in Worship

Leading worship is both a privilege and a burden. The privilege is obvious: there is no time in the week that is more important to individual Christians and to the entire congregation than the hour when the church gathers for corporate worship. The leaders therefore have the unparalleled privilege of guiding God's people into the very presence of Holy Love for spiritual blessing and renewal.

The flip side of this privilege is the burden of high expectations. Worship leaders want the service to go well, whatever that means to the congregation. They want to honor God and to help the people by appropriately prompting and directing them. But when they make a mistake, they feel that every worshiper sees it, hears it, mentally records it and is hindered from genuine worship by it. What a burden to carry every seven days!

Nevertheless, worship leading is a must for ministers. The following ideas have helped me over the years as I have lived between the privilege and the burden.

Prepare yourself. First, as a worship leader I begin by preparing myself for the service. I prepare my spirit early Sunday morning for the most intense spiritual experience of the week. I prepare by praying in silence and solitude. If I do not commit myself and the entire service into the hands of the God who calls me to lead his people in worship, then I have no business standing before the congregation on Sundays and no power for the assignment before me.

I also prepare myself by reviewing my role for the day. I review my sermon in detail early Sunday morning, usually preaching through it one more time to listen for any awkward phrases to delete or any rabbit chasing to avoid.

For me, self-preparation also includes thinking about the prayers I am going to offer that morning, which in my case usually means the pastoral prayer or another specific prayer. I write down in my bulletin any thoughts relating to that particular prayer on that particular day for that particular service. I often take my prayer cues from the words of whatever precedes or follows the time of prayer, such as a Scripture reading, a hymn or special music. That allows the prayer to be an integral part of the service, tied to every other part of worship, not just a stand-alone petition.

Then a few minutes before I go into the sanctuary, I check my appearance one last time. That may sound egotistical or vain, but my goal is to appear neat. I do not want to distract others in worship by my appearance. I avoid gaudy fashions and any clothing or accessories that might draw undue attention to me as the worship leader. I want all eyes to be on Christ, not on me.

Why do I go to all this trouble just to lead people in worship? The answer is simple: nothing else I do all week is as important to the church as leading the people in God-honoring, Christ-centered, Spirit-filled worship. I take my role seriously. After all, "if the trumpet does not sound a clear call, who will get ready for battle?" (1 Cor 14:8).

Be yourself. Since each of us is made in the image of God and is a unique and special reflection of his nature in the world, there is no good reason to try to imitate somebody else. As my college minister Lonnie Hayter used to say, "If you are trying to be like me, then one of us is unnecessary—and I think I know which one it is!" Unfortunately, the desire to imitate is nowhere stronger than in worship leadership, where ministers often try to look and sound like someone other than themselves.

My goal is merely to be myself. That means I try to use my own natural voice, not one that I think might sound more divine! I try to use my own gait, my own gestures, my own wit. That doesn't mean I ignore obvious distracting mannerisms, such as speaking too rapidly, falling into a monotone or putting my hands in my pockets when I preach. But my goal is to understand and to live out what Paul claimed for himself in 1 Corinthians 15:10: "But by the grace of God I am what I am, and his grace to me was not without effect." Let God use your redeemed personality!

Worship for yourself. Few ministerial tasks are more difficult than worshiping God while leading others to worship God. Why? I think it is because worship leaders often want the service to be as mistake-free as possible. As a result, I find it unbearably easy to focus on whether or not the service is running smoothly and according to plan. But in so doing, I fail to focus on the living Christ whom we are there to worship.

I have found a four-part antidote to this problem. First, I remind myself that I planned in advance so that I would not have to worry during the service. That helps me to redirect my attention from the mechanics of the service to God. Second, sometimes I literally lift up my eyes (to the upper back corner of the sanctuary!) while I sing hymns. I imagine that Jesus is there, looking down at us and smiling, and I offer my musical worship to him. Third, I tell the Lord all week long that the sermon is *my* special offering of love and praise to him. That way, on the Sundays when I fail to worship for myself during the first half of the service, I know that at least my preaching can be an act of worship. Finally, I occasionally attend worship services where I have no responsibilities for planning or leadership. I can accomplish this goal, when time permits, by going to occasional chapel services at a nearby Christian university or by attending seasonal services at local churches. Ministers need the opportunity to worship for themselves!

Evaluating the Effectiveness

Ministers who do not evaluate worship services miss the valuable learning experience of improving corporate worship for the glory of God. The first question that arises is who should do this evaluation. I believe that the ministers involved in planning and leading the service should take the initiative in this process. In some churches, lay leaders are involved formally through a worship committee, which meets regularly and offers suggestions to the ministers. In other churches the ministers seek "the view from the pew" on an informal, occasional basis, in order to receive helpful feedback. But the pastor must take the initiative to look carefully at what went well and what went awry in each service.

In seeking the best time for worship evaluation, I have discovered two that I think are not helpful. Immediately after the Sunday service is too soon, because you might be too harsh in your judgment of something that occurred less than an hour earlier. And Thursday or Friday is generally too late, because so much time has elapsed since the service that you may not remember what you were thinking during or immediately after the service. Consequently, I prefer to do my evaluation early in the week, when the service is still fresh in my mind. While I do not elaborately evaluate each element of every service, I do make notes, either written or mental, concerning what I think went well or needs additional attention in every service. Then I share my thoughts with the appropriate ministers.

Consider evaluative questions like these:

☐ Were the facilities and equipment ready? (sound system, lights, air conditioning and so on)

☐ Were the worship leaders fully notified and prepared? (laity and ministers)

☐ Did key lay leaders make any significant comments about the service?

☐ Did each element of worship meet its goal?

☐ Did the *laos* (the people of God) actively participate in worship?

☐ Did the service have an identifiable flow and direction?

☐ Were God's transcendence *and* immanence portrayed?

☐ Did people leave the service aware of God's love, grace and power?

☐ Did people leave knowing that their sins were forgiven?

☐ Did people encounter God in a life-changing way?

Asking these kinds of questions will assist any worship planner with the critical job of worship evaluation. After all, as the old quip goes, whoever fails to learn from the mistakes of the past is doomed to repeat the mistakes of the past.

Epilogue

BABEL OR PENTECOST?

OF ALL OF THE ATTITUDES CHRISTIANS CAN HAVE ABOUT worship styles, the least helpful is a judgmental one. Jesus said, "Do not judge, or you too will be judged" (Mt 7:1). To assume that your worship style is right and that everyone else's is wrong cuts off all fruitful discussion, relegates other worship expressions to the category of uselessness and reveals a case of severe spiritual myopia. We are not permitted to judge the intentions of fellow Christians when they come before God in worship. Nor are we free to look down on the kind of music they sing or the architecture of the building in which they meet. After all, God is simply looking for those who will "worship the Father in spirit and truth" (Jn 4:24). I am not suggesting that we be naive about the possibility of heresy sneaking into church on Sunday mornings. We must always "guard the good deposit that was entrusted" to us (2 Tim 1:14). But the words of Jesus should guide us all in this ongoing, often heated discussion of worship styles: "Be as shrewd as snakes and as innocent as doves" (Mt 10:16).

An often overlooked parable from the New Testament illuminates this whole matter of attitude toward worship styles. In the Gospel of Matthew, Jesus referred to those who have heard about the kingdom of God as being like "the owner of a house who brings out of his storeroom new treasures as well as old" (Mt 13:52). Could it be that the various styles of services cropping up across America reflect something old and something new in worship? Is it possible that the creative Spirit of God is inspiring followers of Jesus Christ to offer both traditional and contemporary expressions of worship "in Spirit and in truth"? Could the resurgence of interest in worship signal a renewal of spirituality and a "hunger and thirst for righteousness"? Is it conceivable that the differences of style highlighted in this book are less a sign of fragmentation than a sign of unity within diversity? Might not this multiplicity of worship experiences stand as a witness to a modern-day Pentecost rather than to the sign of Babel? What would happen if believers stopped judging the way in which their sisters and brothers worship God and instead chose to be grateful for every expression of genuine worship within the larger Christian family?

C. S. Lewis warns against judging other Christians in his preface to *Mere Christianity*. In evaluating the differences between denominations and whether one is more right than another, he describes "mere" Christianity as a "hall out of which doors open into several rooms." He then offers a wise warning which applies to the matter of worship styles as well: "When you have reached your own room, be kind to those who have chosen different doors and to those who are still in the hall. If they are wrong they need your prayers all the more; and if they are your enemies, then you are under orders to pray for them. That is one of the rules common to the whole house."[1]

Therefore may God, whose mystery and majesty demand our praise, remind us that "worship, in all its grades and kinds, is the response of the creature to the Eternal."[2] I believe that all of our attempts to declare the eternal worth of Father, Son and Spirit are pleasing to the One who is worthy. And I encourage all who read these words to bless this doxological diversity and to welcome the New Pentecost that is happening all around us.

"When I Was a Child"

"When I was a child, I talked like a child, I thought like a child, I reasoned like a child. When I became a man, I put childish ways behind me" (1 Cor 13:11). This confession from the apostle Paul gives me great hope. If the most devoted Christian in the early church was able to recognize that some aspects of his earlier life of faith were immature and that he had reached a new vision of following Christ, then I am free to do the same thing. In fact, that is what prompted me to write this book. To go from caring little or nothing about worship to realizing now that it is one of the two or three eternally significant actions in which I engage each week—that is a step of Christian maturity, made possible solely by grace.

Based on my prior experience of growth in the understanding of worship, I have no illusions that I have finally, once and for all, attained the ultimate insights into this amazing divine-human encounter. Nor do I think that this book represents the final word on corporate Christian worship and its various styles. But I do believe that I am going in the right direction, and I hope that you will discover the same meaning and power in worship that I have found.

"Worthy Is the Lamb"

My concluding prayer is that the Spirit of God will so work in the lives of all of us as Jesus' followers that we will come to value worship on earth as it is valued in heaven. For then and there our voices will join "the voice of many angels" (Rev 5:11), singing,

> Worthy is the Lamb, who was slain,
> to receive power and wealth and wisdom and strength
> and honor and glory and praise! . . .

> To him who sits on the throne and to the Lamb
> be praise and honor and glory and power, for ever and ever!
> (Rev 5:12-13)

Notes

Prologue

[1]Sally Morgenthaler, *Worship Evangelism: Inviting Unbelievers into the Presence of God* (Grand Rapids, Mich.: Eerdmans, 1995), p. 38.

Chapter 1: What Is Worship?

[1]Supplied by LaMon Brown, former missionary to India and Thailand and now pastor of First Baptist Church in Montezuma, Georgia.

[2]Ralph P. Martin, *The Worship of God: Some Theological, Pastoral and Practical Reflections* (Grand Rapids, Mich.: Eerdmans, 1982), p. 9.

[3]Robert E. Webber, *Worship Old and New* (Grand Rapids, Mich.: Zondervan, 1982), p. 16.

[4]Horton Davies, *Christian Worship: Its History and Meaning* (Nashville: Abingdon, 1957), p. 105.

[5]As quoted in Franklin M. Segler, *Christian Worship: Its Theology and Practice* (Nashville: Broadman, 1967), p. 4.

Chapter 2: What About Church Growth?

[1]John MacArthur, *The Ultimate Priority* (Chicago: Moody Press, 1983), p. 1.

[2]Kent R. Hunter, "The Quality Side of Church Growth," in *Church Growth: State of the Art*, ed. C. Peter Wagner (Wheaton, Ill.: Tyndale House, 1986), p. 119.

[3]John Piper, *Let the Nations Be Glad! The Supremacy of God in Missions* (Grand Rapids, Mich.: Baker, 1993), p. 11.

[4]Sally Morgenthaler, *Worship Evangelism: Inviting Unbelievers into the Presence of God* (Grand Rapids, Mich.: Eerdmans, 1995), p. 80.

[5]Ibid., pp. 77-78.

Chapter 3: What Are Worship Styles?

[1]Peter Marty, "Beyond the Polarization: Grace and Surprise in Worship," *Christian Century*, March 18-25, 1998, p. 284.

[2]Ibid., p. 285.

[3]Donald P. Hustad, *Jubilate! Church Music in the Evangelical Tradition* (Carol Stream, Ill.: Hope, 1981), p. viii.

Chapter 4: Liturgical Worship

[1]Peter Gilquist, " 'New' Orthodox Attract Evangelicals," *Christianity Today*, May 18, 1992, pp. 50, 53. See also Robert E. Webber, *Evangelicals on the Canterbury*

Trail, reprint ed. (Harrisburg, Penn.: Morehouse, 1989).

[2]This two-part worship pattern is described both in Justin Martyr's *First Apology* (A.D. 140) and in the *Apostolic Tradition* of Hippolytus (A.D. 220). Justin's description of second-century worship is as follows:

> And on the day called Sunday there is a meeting in one place of those who live in the cities or the country, and the memoirs of the apostles or the writings of the prophets are read as long as time permits. When the reader has finished, the president in a discourse urges and invites [us] to the imitation of these noble things. Then we all stand up together and offer prayers. And, as said before, when we have finished the prayer, bread is brought, and wine and water, and the president similarly sends up prayers and thanksgivings to the best of his ability, and the congregation assents, saying the Amen; the distribution, and reception of the consecrated [elements] by each one, takes place and they are sent to the absent by the deacons. (From Cyril Richardson, ed., *Early Christian Fathers* [Philadelphia: Westminster Press, 1953], pp. 287-88, as quoted in Robert E. Webber, *Worship Old and New* [Grand Rapids, Mich.: Zondervan, 1982], p. 49.)

[3]William H. Willimon, *Word, Water, Wine and Bread* (Valley Forge, Penn.: Judson, 1980), p. 77.

[4]The Common Lectionary, which is a book of suggested sermon texts and Scripture readings for each Sunday of the year, is discussed more fully in chapter eleven.

[5]Marva J. Dawn, *Reaching Out Without Dumbing Down: A Theology of Worship for the Turn-of-the-Century Culture* (Grand Rapids, Mich.: Eerdmans, 1995), p. 96.

Chapter 5: Traditional Worship

[1]John Calvin, *Institutes of the Christian Religion*, ed. John T. McNeill, trans. Ford Lewis Battles, Library of Christian Classics 21 (Philadelphia: Westminster Press, 1960), 4.2.2, p. 1042.

[2]Although Separatists and Puritans began their movements in England, they quickly became prominent in early American history. In colonial America, Puritans landed at Massachusetts Bay. They were still Anglicans and are not to be confused with the Mayflower Pilgrims, who were Separatists and who came to Plymouth from exile in the Netherlands.

Chapter 6: Revivalist Worship

[1]James F. White, *Protestant Worship: Traditions in Transition* (Philadelphia: Westminster John Knox, 1989), p. 171.

[2]William H. Willimon, *Word, Water, Wine and Bread* (Valley Forge, Penn.: Judson, 1980), pp. 103-4.

[3]Franklin M. Segler, *Christian Worship: Its Theology and Practice* (Nashville: Broadman, 1967), p. 4.

[4]William H. Willimon, *Worship as Pastoral Care* (Nashville: Abingdon, 1979), pp. 47-48.

Chapter 7: Praise & Worship
[1]Melva Wilson Costen sounds a needed warning against pigeonholing black worship according to popular stereotypes. In *African American Christian Worship* (Nashville: Abingdon, 1993), pp. 15-16, she observes, "Although African Americans share many common worship practices, one should not assume that *all* African American congregations will or should exhibit homogeneous styles of worship. Different situations and circumstances under which exposure to Christianity took place for each congregation, denomination (history and theological orientation), geography, and social life-styles are significant determinants of worship."
[2]Ibid., p. 9.
[3]Ibid., p. 14.
[4]Ibid., p. 77.
[5]See Donald E. Miller, *The Reinventing of American Protestantism: Christianity in the New Millennium* (Berkeley: University of California Press, 1997), and Charles Trueheart, "Welcome to the Next Church," *Atlantic Monthly*, August 1996, pp. 37-58.

Chapter 8: Seeker Service
[1]See Rick Warren, "Designing a Seeker-Sensitive Service," chap. 14 in *The Purpose-Driven Church* (Grand Rapids, Mich.: Zondervan, 1995).

Chapter 9: Choosing a Worship Style
[1]Robert E. Webber, *Signs of Wonder: The Phenomenon of Convergence in Modern Liturgical and Charismatic Churches* (Nashville: StarSong, 1992).
[2]Sally Morgenthaler, *Worship Evangelism: Inviting Unbelievers into the Presence of God* (Grand Rapids, Mich.: Eerdmans, 1995), pp. 130-31.
[3]Steinke draws his inspiration and insights from the seminal work of Edwin H. Friedman's magnum opus on family systems therapy, *Generation to Generation: Family Process in Church and Synagogue* (New York: Guilford, 1985). Steinke's contributions to the discussion are *How Your Church Family Works: Understanding Congregations as Emotional Systems* (New York: Alban Institute, 1993) and *Healthy Congregations: A Systems Approach* (New York: Alban Institute, 1996).
[4]Steinke, *How Your Church Family Works*, p. 124.
[5]Friedman, *Generation to Generation*, p. 229.
[6]C. S. Lewis, *Christian Reflections*, ed. Walter Hooper (Grand Rapids, Mich.: Eerdmans, 1967), pp. 96-97.
[7]See Chip Arn, *How to Start a New Service* (Grand Rapids, Mich.: Baker, 1997).

Chapter 10: Including All of the Elements
[1]Sally Morgenthaler, *Worship Evangelism: Inviting Unbelievers into the Presence of God* (Grand Rapids, Mich.: Eerdmans, 1995), p. 211.
[2]Dietrich Bonhoeffer, *Life Together,* trans. John W. Doberstein (New York: Harper & Row, 1954), p. 61.

[3]B. L. Manning, The Hymns of Wesley and Watts (London: Epworth, 1942), pp. 133-35, as quoted in Ralph P. Martin, The Worship of God: Some Theological, Pastoral and Practical Reflections (Grand Rapids, Mich.: Eerdmans, 1982), p. 46.

[4]Rick Warren, The Purpose-Driven Church (Grand Rapids, Mich.: Zondervan, 1995), pp. 280-81.

[5]Jack Hayford, John Killinger and Howard Stevenson, Mastering Worship (Portland, Ore.: Multnomah Press/Christianity Today, 1990), p. 70.

[6]Martin, Worship of God, p. 31.

[7]Bonhoeffer, Life Together, p. 63.

[8]Ibid., p. 64.

[9]Ibid., p. 62.

[10]Ibid., p. 64.

[11]Ibid., pp. 50-51.

[12]Eugene Peterson, Working the Angles: The Shape of Pastoral Integrity (Grand Rapids, Mich.: Eerdmans, 1987), p. 129.

[13]The Common Lectionary: The Lectionary Proposed by the Consultation on Common Texts (New York: Church Hymnal Corporation, 1983); The Revised Common Lectionary (Nashville: Abingdon, 1992).

[14]Quoted in Horton Davies, Christian Worship: Its History and Meaning (Nashville: Abingdon, 1957), p. 97.

[15]See question 92 of The Westminster Assembly's Shorter Catechism Explained, by Way of Question and Answer, Part 2 (Philadelphia: Presbyterian Board of Education, n.d.), p. 178.

[16]John Calvin, Institutes of the Christian Religion, ed. John T. McNeill, trans. Ford Lewis Battles, Library of Christian Classics 21 (Philadelphia: Westminster Press, 1960), 4.14.1, p. 1277.

[17]Franklin M. Segler, Christian Worship: Its Theology and Practice (Nashville: Broadman, 1967), p. 128.

[18]Robert G. Rayburn, O Come, Let Us Worship: Corporate Worship in the Evangelical Church (Grand Rapids, Mich.: Baker, 1980), p. 249.

[19]Martin, Worship of God, pp. 126-31.

[20]Segler, Christian Worship, p. 147.

[21]Martin, Worship of God, pp. 145-60; and Davies, Christian Worship, pp. 101-2.

Chapter 11: Preparing for Worship

[1]I am especially indebted to Franklin M. Segler, Christian Worship: Its Theology and Practice (Nashville: Broadman, 1967), in this section. It has helped me clarify my own thinking over the years on the topic of worship planning.

[2]Robert E. Webber, Worship Old and New (Grand Rapids, Mich.: Zondervan, 1982), p. 161.

Epilogue

[1]C. S. Lewis, Mere Christianity (Glasgow: Collins/Fontana, 1958), p. 12.

[2]Evelyn Underhill, Worship (New York: Harper, 1936), p. 3.

Suggested Readings

General Introductions to Worship

Davies, J. G., ed. *The Westminster Dictionary of Worship*. Philadelphia: Westminster John Knox, 1979. A masterful, indispensable work, with articles on every subject related to worship.

Martin, Ralph P. *The Worship of God: Some Theological, Pastoral and Practical Reflections*. Grand Rapids, Mich.: Eerdmans, 1982. Filled with New Testament insights on the many dimensions of worship.

Segler, Franklin M. *Christian Worship: Its Theology and Practice*. Nashville: Broadman, 1967. Revised edition edited by Randall Bradley. Nashville: Broadman & Holman, 1996. A classic introduction for those in the Free Church tradition.

Wainwright, Geoffrey. *Doxology: The Praise of God in Worship, Doctrine and Life*. New York: Oxford University Press, 1980. A creative volume on systematic theology as seen through the eyes of worship.

Webber, Robert E. *Worship Old and New*. Grand Rapids, Mich.: Zondervan, 1982; rev. ed. 1994. A groundbreaking book that urges readers to rethink worship theologically.

———, ed. *The Complete Library of Christian Worship*. Nashville: StarSong, 1994. Webber has edited a multivolume encyclopedia on Christian worship that appears to be the most comprehensive attempt yet to describe and interpret the numerous and various aspects of worship. Boasting 650 contributing editors and more than 3,700 pages, this work includes the following individual volumes: *The Biblical Foundations of Christian Worship; Twenty Centuries of Christian Worship; The Renewal of Sunday Worship; Music and the Arts in Worship* (2 volumes); *The Services of the Christian Year; The Sacred Actions of Worship;* and *The Ministries of Christian Worship.*

White, James F. *Introduction to Christian Worship*. Nashville: Abingdon, 1980. A classic introduction for those in the mainline churches.

Willimon, William H. *The Service of God: How Worship and Ethics Are Related*. Nashville: Abingdon, 1983. A fresh restatement of worship from the perspective of Christian ethics.

———. *Worship as Pastoral Care*. Nashville: Abingdon, 1979. An important look at how worship functions within the fellowship of a church.

Worship in the Bible

Cullmann, Oscar. *Early Christian Worship*. London: SCM Press, 1953. A brief but penetrating look at several aspects of New Testament worship.

Martin, Ralph P. "Worship." In *The International Standard Bible Encyclopedia*, 4:1117-33. Edited by Geoffrey W. Bromiley. 4 vols. Grand Rapids, Mich.: Eerdmans, 1979-1988. Unusually instructive and comprehensive.

————. *Worship in the Early Church*. Grand Rapids, Mich.: Eerdmans, 1964. The most insightful technical study of New Testament worship I have read.

Rowley, H. H. *Worship in Ancient Israel: Its Forms and Meanings*. Philadelphia: Fortress, 1967. Good overview of Old Testament worship.

Worship in Christian History

Costen, Melva Wilson. *African American Christian Worship*. Nashville: Abingdon, 1993. One of the most helpful recent volumes on black worship in America.

Davies, Horton. *Christian Worship: Its History and Meaning*. Nashville: Abingdon, 1957. Easy reading, very rewarding.

Maxwell, William D. *An Outline of Christian Worship*. New York: Oxford University Press, 1936. A true classic.

White, James F. *A Brief History of Christian Worship*. Nashville: Abingdon, 1993. Solid, substantial, succinct.

————. *Protestant Worship: Traditions in Transition*. Philadelphia: Westminster John Knox, 1989. The most thorough book I have read on Protestant worship history.

Willimon, William H. *Word, Water, Wine and Bread*. Valley Forge, Penn.: Judson, 1980. The best short history of worship available.

Worship Styles

Basden, Paul. " 'Something Old, Something New': Worship Styles for Baptists in the Nineties." In *Ties That Bind: Life Together in the Baptist Vision*, pp. 171-90. Edited by Gary A. Furr and Curtis W. Freeman. Macon, Ga.: Smyth & Helwys, 1994.

————. "Worship with Integrity." In *Honest Numbers: Growing Churches with Integrity*. Edited by Robert M. Parham. Nashville: Baptist Center for Christian Ethics, 1995. These two works are my first attempts at differentiating worship styles.

Edwards, Mark D. *Exalt His Name Together*. Nashville: Convention, 1994. Edwards describes five styles of worship also, but he substitutes "blended" for my "revivalist."

Towns, Elmer. *Putting an End to Worship Wars*. Nashville: Broadman & Holman, 1997. Towns delineates six "paradigms" of worship: the evangelistic church, the Bible-expositional church, the renewal church, the body-life church, the liturgical church and the congregational church. These paradigms are not identical to worship styles, but they certainly overlap.

Webber, Robert E. "From Jerusalem to Willow Creek." *Discipleship Journal* 70 (1992): 42-47. A seminal work that differentiates six "contemporary models of worship": liturgical worship, traditional Protestant worship, praise and worship, creative worship, seeker service/believers worship and convergence worship.

————. *Signs of Wonder: The Phenomenon of Convergence in Modern Liturgical and Charismatic Churches.* Nashville: StarSong, 1992. This book has been revised and reprinted as *Blended Worship: Achieving Substance and Relevance in Worship.* Peabody, Mass.: Hendrickson, 1994. Webber encourages liturgical and charismatic churches to "cross-pollinate" their worship experiences.

Willis, Charles. " 'Blended' Worship Combines Traditional, Contemporary." *Facts and Trends,* October 1993, p. 1.

————. "Praise, Worship Lead to God, Minister of Music Says." *Facts and Trends,* October 1993, p. 6.

————. " 'Seeker' Worship Style Targets the Unchurched." *Facts and Trends,* October 1993, p. 7.

————. "Traditional SBC Worship: Informal Dignity." *The Baptist Standard,* September 1, 1993, p. 13. These four companion articles are early attempts at categorizing worship styles in Baptist life.

Liturgical Worship

The Common Lectionary: The Lectionary Proposed by the Consultation on Common Texts. New York: Church Hymnal Corporation, 1983.

The Revised Common Lectionary. Nashville: Abingdon, 1992.

Contemporary Music in Worship

Frame, John M. *Contemporary Worship Music: A Biblical Defense.* Phillipsburg, N.J.: Presbyterian & Reformed, 1997. Reformed theologian and musician answers objections to use of contemporary music in worship.

Hustad, Donald P. *Jubilate! Church Music in the Evangelical Tradition.* Carol Stream, Ill.: Hope, 1981.

————. *Jubilate II: Church Music in Worship and Renewal.* Carol Stream, Ill.: Hope, 1993. Former organist for Billy Graham crusades makes plea for openness to new styles of music without rejecting classical hymnody.

Liesch, Barry. *The New Worship: Straight Talk on Music and the Church.* Grand Rapids, Mich.: Baker, 1996. Music professor praises contemporary music while still affirming value of hymns.

Miller, Steve. *The Contemporary Music Debate: Worldly Compromise or Agent of Renewal?* Wheaton, Ill.: Tyndale House, 1993. An unapologetic defense of the value of contemporary Christian music in worship.

Seeker Services

Dawn, Marva J. *Reaching Out Without Dumbing Down: A Theology of Worship for the Turn-of-the-Century Culture.* Grand Rapids, Mich.: Eerdmans, 1996. A scathing critique of the seeker-sensitive approach of blending worship and evangelism.

Dobson, Ed. *Starting a Seeker-Sensitive Service.* Grand Rapids, Mich.: Zondervan, 1993. A clear description by a leading practitioner.

Hunter, George G., III. *Church for the Unchurched.* Nashville: Abingdon, 1996. A seminary professor gives "two enthusiastic thumbs up" to the effectiveness of the seeker service as an evangelistic tool.

Morgenthaler, Sally. *Worship Evangelism: Inviting Unbelievers into the Presence of God.* Grand Rapids, Mich.: Zondervan, 1995. Morgenthaler offers "three cheers" for seeker services, but she redefines what seekers are looking for when they attend worship.

Pritchard, Gregory A. *Willow Creek Seeker Services: Evaluating a New Way of Doing Church.* Grand Rapids, Mich.: Baker, 1995. A sympathetic treatment of seeker services.

Warren, Rick. *The Purpose-Driven Church.* Grand Rapids, Mich.: Zondervan, 1995. Part four describes the Saddleback concept of seeker-sensitive worship.

Planning & Leading Worship

Flamming, Peter James. "The Pastor as Worship Planner." In *Baptist Faith and Witness: The Papers of the Study and Research Division of the Baptist World Alliance 1990-1995.* Birmingham, Ala.: Samford University Press, 1996. Excellent primer on the pastor's role on Sunday mornings.

Furr, Gary A., and Milburn Price. *The Dialogue of Worship: Creating Space for Revelation and Response.* Macon, Ga.: Smyth & Helwys, 1998. An experienced pastor converses with a veteran church music professor and minister of music about the divine-human dialogue of worship.

Hayford, Jack, John Killinger and Howard Stevenson. *Mastering Worship.* Portland, Ore.: Multnomah Press/Christianity Today, 1990. Three practicing ministers write about the "how to" of worship leadership.

Ortlund, Anne. *Up with Worship: How to Quit Playing Church.* Ventura, Calif.: Regal, 1975. Wise and witty, with some practical pointers for making worship more meaningful.

Siewert, Alison, ed., with Andy Crouch, Matt Frazier and Sundee Frazier. *Worship Team Handbook.* Downers Grove, Ill.: InterVarsity Press, 1998. Members of the Urbana worship team compile insights from their own experience on how to plan and lead contemporary services.

Stevenson, Howard. "Architect of Worship." *Leadership,* Winter 1996, pp. 103-6. Helpful and practical advice on planning services.